SILENT THREADS:

A PRISONER OF CHAOS

Reclaim Discipline. Redefine Masculinity.
Rise from the Darkness.

BY ERIC M. KILCULLEN

"There's no resurrection without ruin."

Silent Threads: A Prisoner of Chaos
Reclaim Discipline, Redefine Masculinity,
and Rise from the Darkness

For permissions or inquiries, contact:
Ink & Armour Publishing
command@reigninsilence.com

ISBN Hardcover: 979-8-9986555-3-1
ISBN Paperback: 979-8-9986555-0-0
ISBN E-Book: 979-8-9986555-5-5

First Edition

Printed in the United States of America
Published by Ink & Armour Publishing

An imprint of Mr. & Mrs. Krush, LLC

FOREWORD

Within these pages lies a collection of truths—sharpened in the quietest storms and forged in the deepest chaos.

Each thread is a shard of lived experience, rebellion, and reflection. These are not simply words—they are survival instincts, battle scars, and wisdom distilled.

This is not a book for the faint-hearted.
It is a weapon—designed for those navigating the trenches of life.

It's not poetry. It's not a memoir.
It's doctrine—cut down into truths, creeds, and codes. Each one stands on its own... but ties into a larger war—**the war within**.

This book is broken into five crucibles—each chapter a pillar: **Chaos. Hardship. Survival. Manipulation. Freedom.**

What follows is more than ink.
It is a map—forged in silence, etched through suffering.

DEDICATION—THE FIRST THREAD

To my mother—who bled to give me life. Who taught me that stillness is not weakness—it's readiness. That presence is louder than pride. And that love, real love, does not coddle—it forges.

To CMSgt Jack C.L. Ashley (1943–2010)—who taught me that silence isn't weakness—it's control. A warrior of few words and iron presence.

He never had to raise his voice. Because he already carried the weight of command.

To every soldier, leader, and builder forged in fire, tempered in stillness, and sharpened in shadows where no one applauded—this book is for you. You are seen.

You are honored. And now... you are armed.

— E.K. ~*Mr. Krush*

CONTENTS

INTRODUCTION

In the absence of noise, we hear the truth: uncomfortable, unfiltered, and unforgiving. Silence has always been my greatest weapon, my harshest teacher, and my only reliable ally. It does not comfort; it confronts. It tears apart illusions, drowns excuses, and leaves only raw potential waiting to be harnessed.

Every generation forgets the same truth: everything you need is already inside you. You don't need permission to rise. You don't need praise to continue. You don't need comfort to grow. What you need is to listen—truly listen—to the silence beneath the chaos.

This book does not offer peace; peace is temporary and often false. It is not a promise of shortcuts or a celebration of hollow victories. It is a confrontation. A mirror. A demand.

It will force you to confront your chaos. To survive it, command it, and eventually transcend it. It will hold a mirror to your potential and ask why you've let it molder. It will expose the very threads you refuse to untangle—threads woven by fear, ego, and comfort. These quotes are not stitched together for the sake of inspiration; they are scars forged from battles that most never witness.

I do not seek your agreement. I seek your discomfort—for only in discomfort can you grow beyond the complacency that made you prisoner to the very chaos you've mistaken for control.

There is no mercy here. No excuses. Only weapons: sharp, simple, brutally effective.

But you must wield them. I cannot do the work for you. No one can.

To the leader suffocating in silence.

To the entrepreneur lost in hunger.

To the warrior dulled by ease.

This is your map through the storm. This is your reckoning. Welcome to the edge of tomorrow—step closer, where hesitation dies and purpose begins.

Read slowly. Reflect deeply. Interpret freely. Survive relentlessly.

And when you're ready—break free.

— Mr. Krush

FROM BLOOD TO INK

I did not write this in peace.
I wrote it at 2:17 a.m., sitting on the edge of my bed, fully dressed for a day I had no intention of showing up for.

The mask was broken.
I was not grieving.
I was drowning in entitlement, filled with pointless pity.
Sullen, wrapped in disgust—because deep down, I thought I deserved better than the consequences I helped create.

I had just been cast out by people I once bled for.
Blamed for things I did not do.
Cut off without trial or truth.
And for a while, I wore that wound like it was my identity.

I fell on the very sword I swore to protect.
Not because I was weak—
But because I was loyal. **Blinded by the desperation for approval.**
And in the end, I paid for it in silence, not in honor.

That's the part most men will not admit—
That sometimes we break **not because we are weak,**
But because we gave everything, and still lost.

But loss is not the end.
It is the start of the reckoning.

I did not heal in silence.
I bled in it.

So no—this is not a book.
It is a blueprint I carved from my own collapse.
It is the scar I earned from turning a wound into something **worth carrying**.

Every line in here is a version of me I executed:
The pleaser. The performer.
**The one who waited for justice and begged for forgiveness—
instead of becoming the monster under the chaos.**

I do not need your agreement.
I need your honesty.

If you have been cast out, doubted, dismissed—good.
That means you are exactly where fire begins.

Take what you need.
But take it seriously.
This is not ink.
It is—blood.

1

THE PREDATOR OF CHAOS —
THE SILENCE IN EVERY STORM

Silence isn't passive. It's not absence.
It's posture. A stance of those who already understand the rules—and refuse to play by them.

Chaos screams. It has to.
It shouts to be noticed, scrambles to disrupt, spins in circles, begging for reaction.
Because chaos is loud for one reason: **it fears what doesn't flinch.**

Power doesn't raise its voice. It doesn't beg to be seen.
It observes. It calculates. It waits.
And when the moment is right, it doesn't announce the strike—**it just hits. Once.**
No warning. No permission.

That's why silence is terrifying. Not because it's empty—
but because it's loaded.
Charged with clarity.
Backed by purpose.
Weighted with restraint.

The roar isn't the threat.

The real threat is what watches while you're distracted.

The apex doesn't bark.

It doesn't argue.

It doesn't defend itself with noise.

It just moves. And the whole system shifts.

Silence is the predator.

Chaos is just the bait.

SILENT AXIOM I

"Silence remains the predator to chaos."
— *Silent Threads*

The Echo Fears the Origin

Power doesn't raise its voice. It raises the standard.

Meaning:
Chaos feeds on attention. It thrives on noise, panic, and performance.
Without reaction, it withers.

Hidden Meaning:
Silence isn't absence—it's authority.
It's presence restrained.
It's power refined until it no longer needs permission to act.

Message:
Silence doesn't shout.
It studies.
It waits.
It hunts in the stillness—
and when it moves,
it doesn't miss.

I. The Loudest One Isn't the Apex

Chaos always tries to be the main character.
It makes noise.
Throws shadows.
Demands you look.

But real power doesn't flinch when provoked.
The strongest one in the room?
It's the one who hasn't moved—yet.

Because the apex doesn't announce itself.
It chooses its moment.
And when it strikes—
the noise never had a chance.

II. Silence Is the Sharpest Weapon

Not every war is fought with steel.
Some are won by the one who speaks last—
or never.

Silence holds pressure.
It holds tension.
And when the time is right—
it doesn't burst.
It cuts.

Quiet isn't peace.
Quiet is preparation.
And if you're not ready for stillness—
you're not ready for war.

III. Chaos Starves Without Reaction

The goal of chaos isn't destruction—
it's attention.

It wants to be fed.
Fed by panic.
Fed by confusion.
Fed by noise.

But when you give it nothing?
It starts eating itself.

Chaos can't grow in calm.
It can't survive in presence.
It needs drama to stay alive.
So starve it.
Starve it with stillness.

IV. Harriet Tubman Moved in Silence

She didn't campaign.
She didn't command armies.
She didn't wait for permission.

She moved—through swamps, shadows, and death.
Again and again.

She didn't shout at enemies.
She slipped past them.
Quiet.
Ruthless.

Unstoppable.

She didn't lead by volume.
She led by vision.

"I never ran my train off the track, and I never lost a passenger."
— *Harriet Tubman, 1869*

That wasn't luck.
That was silence—mastered.

V. The Predator of Chaos
"Silence remains the predator to chaos."
— *Silent Threads*

Real power doesn't respond to provocation.
It doesn't roar to be seen.
It doesn't argue with noise.

It listens.
It calculates.
And when the time comes—
it moves once.

No warning.
No hesitation.
No applause needed.

That's why chaos fears silence.
Because silence doesn't fight it—

it ends it.

Final Confrontation

In this world, silence isn't just power—
it's survival.

It is the unshakable foundation of leadership, motivation, and discipline.
It is the **quiet crown of dominance—**
first over the self,
then over the world.

SILENT AXIOM II

"To shun adventure is to deny yourself a life worth living. Stagnation is the slowest form of decay."
— *Silent Threads*

The Death Hidden in Comfort
Complacency is the tomb where greatness rests.

Meaning:
A life without risk or challenge hollows itself out—
until nothing is left but routine that looks like peace
but feels like decay.

Hidden Meaning:
Comfort isn't safety—it's sedation.
You don't notice you're dying when you're not moving.
But the stillness rots everything.

Message:
Living isn't surviving.
It's choosing the road that demands something from you.
Adventure isn't luxury.
It's oxygen.

I. Safety Isn't What You Think It Is

You were told to stay safe.
To choose stability.
To find a rhythm—and never leave it.

But safety, unchecked, becomes a tomb.
And predictability?
It's a padded cell made of "just fine."

The people who rot the fastest?
Aren't the reckless—
they're the ones who stopped choosing.

II. Adventure Is the Fire That Keeps You from Going Numb

Adventure isn't cliff diving or passport stamps.
It's anything that demands a new version of you.

That conversation you've avoided.
That business you haven't started.
That future you're scared to meet.

Avoiding that path?
It's not wise.
It's slow death dressed as safety.
You're building your own ceiling—
and calling it protection.

III. Stagnation Is a Slow Burial

It doesn't feel like death at first.
It feels like rest.

Routine.
Familiarity.

But day by day—
your instincts dull.
Your edge softens.
Your fire fades.

Until one day you wake up
and realize you haven't moved in years.
Not physically.
Spiritually.

IV. Amelia Earhart Chose the Sky

They told her to stay grounded.
That the air wasn't made for women.
That her path was foolish.

She flew anyway.
Not because it was safe —
but because it was hers.

"Adventure is worthwhile in itself."
— *Amelia Earhart*

She didn't die chasing fame.
She died chasing freedom.
And there's no better ending than that.

V. The Death Hidden in Comfort
"To shun adventure is to deny yourself a life worth living."
— *Silent Threads*

You weren't built for stillness.
You weren't made for the shallow end.

Avoiding adventure?
It isn't maturity—it's surrender.

You trade your fire for furniture.
You become the best-dressed version of regret.

The moment you stop seeking?
That's when you start fading.

The cure?
Movement.
Risk.
Growth.
Discomfort—by choice.
Because comfort doesn't keep you safe.
It keeps you weak.
And weakness has never earned — legacy.

SILENT AXIOM III

"You cannot understand the depths of violence without first mastering the power of silence."
— *Silent Threads*

The Violence Hidden in Stillness

Without silence, force becomes chaos.
With silence, it becomes war.

Meaning:

Violence, at its highest form, is not emotional—it is precision. It is the quiet, calculated execution of intent.

Hidden Meaning:

Silence isn't the opposite of violence—it's its architect.
It teaches control, observation, restraint—and sharpens force into mastery.

Message:

Violence without silence is reaction.
Violence with silence is command.

I. The World Mistakes Chaos for Strength

We're told violence is loud.

That rage is power.

That whoever swings first—wins.

But chaos is just noise with adrenaline.

It lacks timing. Precision. Vision.

True violence doesn't announce itself.

It doesn't warn.

It waits.

It measures.

Then it ends you.

II. Silence Is the Blade Before the Strike

Silence is where your instincts sharpen.

It's the space where emotion gets filtered.

Where impulse is broken into choice.

Every deadly warrior knows:

What you don't do — is just as powerful as what you do.

Silence is your breath before the shot.

The pause before the punch.

The decision to wait until your enemy makes the first mistake—then turn it into their last.

III. Violence Without Discipline Becomes Self-Destruction

Without silence, you react.

You panic.

You swing wildly and loudly—and bleed yourself dry.

Anger doesn't win wars.

Clarity does.
You don't act because you're provoked—
you act because you've chosen.
Every movement is intention.
Every strike is a message.
And every message lands.

IV. Musashi Waited for the Mistake
Miyamoto Musashi.
Samurai. Duelist.
Unbeaten in over sixty life-or-death fights.
He didn't fight with speed.
He fought with silence.
He studied rhythm.
Watched breath.
Let his enemies burn out their fear with noise.
And when the rhythm broke—
he struck once.
That was all it took.

To win any battle, you must fight as if you are already dead."
— Miyamoto Musashi, The Book of Five Rings

He didn't perform.
He calculated.
That's what true violence looks like:
Still.
Precise.
Absolute.

V. The Violence Hidden in Stillness

"You cannot understand the depths of violence without first mastering the power of silence."
— *Silent Threads*

Power isn't just in the blow—it's in the decision not to throw it.
Violence without silence is childish.
Violence with silence is surgical.

The loud one flails.
The still one ends it.

You don't need rage.
You need readiness.
And readiness comes from silence:
Not the absence of action—
but the discipline to wait until action becomes unstoppable.

The world tells you to fear violence.
But the wise?
They fear the one who speaks last.
Who breathes slowly.
Who sees everything—
and says nothing.

Because when they move—it's not aftermath. It's calculated carnage, etched in bone—and paid in blood.

SILENT AXIOM IV

"Where you see change, I discovered growth."
— *Silent Threads*

The Evolution Hidden in Adaptation
Change breaks the weak.
It builds the ready.

Meaning:
Change happens outside of you. Growth happens because of you.

Hidden Meaning:
Change is noise. Growth is signal. Most react to the shift. Few use it to evolve.

Message:
Discomfort isn't a threat—
it's a mirror.
And what you do next decides who you become.

I. Change Isn't the Enemy—Your Reaction Is

Most people flinch when the ground moves.
They brace, curse, panic—waiting for things to "go back."
But that version of the world is gone.

And the ones who survive?
Are the ones who stop asking for normal—
and start building something better.

Change doesn't destroy you.
It exposes you.
And if you're paying attention,
it invites you to rise.

II. Growth Is the Violence You Choose

Growth isn't passive.
It's not some gentle expansion.

It's violent.
Uncomfortable.
Surgical.

It rips the false version of you out by the roots
so something real can take its place.

Change creates the conditions.
Growth requires the decision.

Not to flinch.
Not to freeze.

To adapt—
without apology.

III. The Earth Doesn't Stop Spinning for You
You don't get points for staying the same.
You don't get crowns for clinging to comfort.

The world doesn't pause just because you're not ready.
Change doesn't ask for your approval—it keeps moving.

And if you don't move with it,
you'll rot where you stand.

Adaptation isn't betrayal.
It's responsibility.
It's leadership.
It's survival.

The people who fall the hardest?
Aren't the weakest.

They're the ones who thought yesterday's strength
would survive tomorrow's storm.

If you won't evolve—
you will vanish.

If you won't shift—
you will break.

Grow. Or be left behind.
Because the Earth?
It doesn't stop spinning for you.

IV. Darwin Didn't Worship the Strong
He never said survival belongs to the strongest.
He said it belongs to the ones who adapt.

Not the loudest.
Not the smartest.
The ones most aligned with reality—whatever shape it takes.

"The ones who survive are not the strongest or most intelligent,
but the ones most responsive to change."
— *interpreted from Charles Darwin*

Growth doesn't need you to be perfect.
It just needs you to stop pretending you're safe.

V. The Evolution Hidden in Adaptation
"Where you see change, I discovered growth."
— *Silent Threads*

When others freeze—you flex.
When they stall—you sharpen.
Because change doesn't break warriors.
It reveals them.

Change is just the event.

Growth is your response.
So when the ground shifts—move.

When the door locks—tear it from the frame.
And when they ask how you outlived what broke them?
Don't say you endured.
Say you evolved.
Then bare your teeth—
and remind them:
you weren't made to just survive...
you were built to THRIVE.

SILENT AXIOM V

"Life's forks are conquered best with allies."
— *Silent Threads*

Brotherhood Is Born in Battle

Lone wolves starve. Packs survive.

Meaning:

No one makes it through alone. At every crossroad, your strength multiplies by who walks beside you.

Hidden Meaning:

Allies aren't luxury—they're legacy. They don't just help you carry weight; they decide how far you go.

Message:

Discipline is contagious.

Loyalty is lethal.

And you will go further with five wolves than one sword.

I. The Lone Wolf Is a Myth

You've seen the posters.

Heard the slogans.

"Alpha. Lone wolf. Walk alone."

Myth.

In nature, the lone wolf doesn't lead—

it limps.

It's injured. Exiled. Dying.

The strongest don't hunt alone.

They hunt with a pack.

They feed together. Bleed together.

Win together.

The lone wolf doesn't conquer.

It survives—until it doesn't.

II. The Pack Is the Armor You Don't See

When the road splits, pressure comes.

And pressure breaks the isolated.

But the one surrounded by allies?

Doesn't flinch.

Doesn't guess.

He gathers intel. Holds counsel. Strikes clean.

A real ally won't flatter you.

They'll challenge your fire.

They'll remind you of the standard

when you're too tired to hold it yourself.

III. Loyalty Is a Weapon

People think loyalty is softness.

That it means comfort, validation, praise.

No.

Loyalty is war.

It's knowing who you'd bleed for—

and who'd bleed for you.

It's not built through words.

It's built in fires. In fights. In forks.

True loyalty doesn't mean agreement.

It means presence.

The kind that doesn't vanish when it gets hard.

IV. Marcus Aurelius Never Stood Alone

He wasn't just a Roman emperor.

He was a warrior. A philosopher.

But above all—he chose wisely who stood beside him.

He kept generals, scholars, soldiers—

people who weren't afraid to speak truth to the throne.

"When you arise in the morning, think of what a privilege it
is to be alive—to think, to enjoy, to love."
— *Marcus Aurelius*, Meditations

Even the most disciplined man in history
didn't walk alone.

There's honor in dying for loyalty—
but you rarely discover legacy, alone.

V. Brotherhood Is Born in Battle

"Life's forks are conquered best with allies."

— *Silent Threads*

When the road splits,

don't just ask which way to go—

ask who's going with you.

Because paths don't make you stronger.

People do.

The ones who stay when others run.

The ones who challenge you without needing credit.

The ones who see your fire fading—

and guard it with their own.

Loyalty is not weakness. It's strategy.

And if you want to go far?

You better bleed with a pack that won't break.

CHAPTER CLOSING: THE QUIET CROWN

From the depths of Silence—We Rise.
Through Unity—We Reign.

This chapter begins where all warriors must start: with silence, discipline, and the choice to walk into chaos without announcing your presence. But no warrior conquers alone. The path ahead is not simply walked; it is forged by the silent, the disciplined, and the loyal. Those who choose not only to fight, but to fight together. Victory is never the fruit of isolated strength. It is born from the unspoken trust between those who shoulder the weight together—warriors who understand that solitude is strategy, but unity is force. It is the disciplined who sharpen each other. It is the loyal who hold the line when others fold. And it is the wise who know that the greatest battles are never won alone. The road ahead widens into uncertainty, but now it is no longer walked alone. It is commanded by those who stand together. You've spent enough time in rooms trying to be heard. Enough breath on arguments that needed no answer. Enough energy reacting to things that never deserved your fire.

Now you know better. You've learned what chaos hates most: stillness. Not passivity. Presence. Because chaos feeds on motion, on noise, on performance. It expects you to flinch. To explain. To respond. But the apex doesn't respond. It waits. It watches. And then—it moves once. With purpose. With force. With no need for a second strike.

I. Alexander the Great — The Silence That Conquered the World

He was born in 356 BCE, in Pella—the capital of ancient
Macedonia.
Son of King Philip II.
Student of Aristotle.
Raised in fire.
Fed by philosophy.

By twenty, he wore the crown.
By thirty, he had carved his name into the bones of the world.

But it wasn't rage that made him lethal—
it was restraint.
He didn't win because he was loud.
He won because he moved with the weight of silence.

Before battle, he withheld.
Held formation.
Let fear rot the hearts of his enemies until they broke before he swung a sword.
When his army hesitated in the deserts of India,
he didn't command them.
He walked alone—forward.
And they followed.

"There is nothing impossible to him who will try."
— *Alexander the Great, as recorded by Arrian, Anabasis Alexandri*

He wasn't just a conqueror—he was a chameleon.
Wore the robes of his enemies.
Married into their bloodlines.

Absorbed their gods.

Not to become them—
But to prove he could become more.

He didn't just master violence—he transcended it.
Carried the weight of his mistakes,
including the blood of his closest friend.

And that silence—that grief —
was louder than any crown.

Alexander didn't perform.
Didn't seek applause.
He moved once—and the world bent.

II. Nims Purja — The Mountain Doesn't Care If You Scream

Born in Myagdi, Nepal—raised in the kind of altitude that strips away ego.
Son of a Gurkha.
Special forces operator.
Trained to disappear.
Built in silence.

After war, he didn't rest—he climbed.
Not just mountains—**death zones.**
Where most can't breathe,
he breathed deeper.

In 2019, he set out to do what no one had done:
Summit all fourteen of Earth's 8,000-meter peaks—
in one climbing season.
He did it in six months and six days.

"I wanted to show what was possible."
— *Nims Purja*, Beyond Possible

No banners.
No self-congratulation.
No drama.
Just movement.
Just oxygen shared with dying climbers.
Just quiet.
Just team.

Just truth in motion.

He knew violence—not of war, but of wind, ice, and gravity.
He stared down avalanches, watched others fall,
and still moved—without panic, without pause.

He didn't climb for records.
He climbed for legacy.

For the invisible giants who carried others to the top and never got
credit. The Sherpas.
His brothers.

And when he reached the final summit?
No speech.

No scream.

Just two words:

"Job done."

III. Final Reflection — The Apex Doesn't Announce Itself

One led armies through dust and blood.

One led brothers through ice and silence.

Both moved without volume.

Both struck without warning.

Both proved:

Chaos is not defeated by noise—it's outlasted by clarity.

Alexander didn't wait for consensus.

He didn't ask to lead.

He became the reason others followed.

Nims didn't ask permission to challenge death.

He walked into it with a team,

a mission,

and a pulse so still

the mountain couldn't shake it.

They weren't loud.

They were aligned.

That's what you've been missing.

Not power—**presence.**

Not talent—**timing.**

Not strength—**stillness.**

...

Let the loud chase attention.
Let the crowd mistake motion for power.
Let the chaos scream its truth to the void.

You?
You move differently now.

You've learned what silence really is:
strategy.
sovereignty.
The calm behind the strike.

You don't flinch.
You don't explain.
You don't perform.

You prepare.

And when it's time—
you act.
With precision.
With purpose.
With nothing left to prove.

Because in the end—
he loud may echo.
But only the quiet ever command.

So when chaos knocks again, welcome it like an old rival.
Don't flinch. Don't explain. Just move.
One strike. One shift. That's all it takes.
Because silence doesn't fight for control—
it commands the battlefield before the war drums begin.

2

BROKEN & BOUND

Shattered by Comfort. Empowered by Pain.

There's never been a warrior who hasn't felt the weight of invisible chains. Not all prisons have bars. Some are built in silence—forged from fear, regret, complacency, or betrayal. The worst part? Most people don't even notice the cuffs tightening until they can barely move.

This chapter isn't about avoiding the chains. It's about facing them. Broken & bound isn't the story of weakness. It's the cost of necessary suffering.

Strength is never gifted. It isn't found in books, borrowed from slogans, or passed down through rituals. It's built—slowly, painfully, and almost always alone. The greatest warriors aren't the ones who avoid breaking. They're the ones who rebuild from the breach and forge the fragments into armor.

Life *will* bind you. That's not a warning—that's law. You'll be bent, cut, and broken by forces you never asked for. But here's the harsh truth: most of the damage you'll carry? *You* did that. Through wasted time. Through excuses. Through lowered standards. Through pretending you were less than you are.

Some chains were forced on you by others. But the strongest ones? You welded them in silence—when no one was watching.

Discipline doesn't grow when everything works. It's forged in the moments nothing does. It lives between breaking and rebuilding. Leadership isn't tested when the water is calm. It's revealed when the ship is split in half and sinking. Anyone can act bold when nothing is on the line. But when life collapses under you—when it strips you down and shows you the mirror—that's where real leaders are born.

In the dark.

Unseen.

Alone.

Some chains are old debts you've avoided. Others were left by cowards who wore strength like a mask—and you still carry their mark while they wear your pain like a crown. But the most dangerous chains? You put those on the day you chose comfort over growth. The day you traded discomfort for denial. Revenge. Wasted potential. Bitterness. Silence when you should have spoken. These are the links. And while we're busy blaming the world, we miss the enemy that's been inside the whole time.

Your first opponent isn't any of the ones who betrayed you. It's the version of you that lowered the standard—and called it survival.

This chapter is your invitation to face that opponent. No easy answers. No shortcuts. No applause. Discipline doesn't pretend the chains aren't there. It sees them clearly, snaps them one link at a time, and refuses to wear them again.

There is no freedom without first being bound.

Those who say otherwise aren't free—they're just comfortably caged.

SILENT AXIOM VI

"If it's revenge you're after, begin with the version of you who betrayed your potential."
— *Silent Threads*

The Ultimate Betrayal—Revenge Buried in Responsibility

Revenge is not rage—it's resurrection.

Meaning:

The one who hurt your future the most was you. The only way forward is to bury the coward who did.

Hidden Meaning:

Revenge isn't power taken from your enemies—it's power reclaimed from your former self.
The version of you that chose comfort, fear, and smallness.
You don't need vengeance.
You need evolution.

Message:

Before you chase them—face yourself.
Because until you do, you're still their prisoner.

I. Revenge Haunts Your Scars

Your reflection demands a reckoning.
We're taught that revenge is a weapon—a comeback, a firestorm.
But most people aren't after justice.
They're just bleeding from their own choices.

They blame the world. Their past. Their ex. Their enemies.
But the truth?

The first betrayal came from inside.
You missed the reps.
You skipped the hard route.
You chose what felt good over what made you sharp.

So before you make a hit list—
make a mirror list.

II. The Architect of Your Chains

Every excuse.
Every wasted morning.
Every silence you chose when you should've spoken—
they welded links in your chain.

It wasn't them.
It wasn't fate.
It was *you*.
Building your own captivity,
one soft decision at a time.

And now you want revenge?
Then start with demolition.

Burn down the version of yourself who built this prison.

III. Revenge Without Discipline Is Just a Tantrum

Without direction, revenge turns into obsession.
It's loud. It's reactive. It's weak.

True vengeance isn't about getting even—
it's about never being beneath them again.

You don't post it.
You don't shout it.
You don't chase it.
You become it.

IV. Fridtjof Nansen Walked into the Ice

Born in 1861, Nansen was a scientist. A statesman.
But before all that—he was a man no one believed in.

He set out to reach the North Pole—not for glory,
but to prove that "impossible" was just a word.

When everyone else sailed west,
he sailed north.

He let his ship freeze into the Arctic,
then walked into the unknown—

not to conquer nature,
but to conquer himself.

"The difficult is what takes a little time.
The impossible is what takes a little longer."
— *Fridtjof Nansen*

He didn't scream for revenge against doubt.
He just moved.
Deliberate. Cold. Unstoppable.

**He buried the version of himself who might have listened to fear—
under ice.**

V. The Revenge Buried in Responsibility
**"If it's revenge you're after, begin with the version of you who
betrayed your potential."**
— *Silent Threads*

Don't chase the enemy who hurt you.
Erase the self who let them.

You don't need applause.
You don't need validation.
You need action—
measured, disciplined, absolute.

Because revenge isn't loud.
It's surgical.
It's not fury.

It's focus.

And once you've made peace with the war inside?
They can't touch you anymore.
Because you've already buried
the only one who ever could.

Not every strike requires an iron fist.
The wisest warriors conquer without lifting a blade—they master the art of control.

SILENT AXIOM VII

"Even the sharpest teeth cannot bite water."
— *Silent Threads*

The Unbreakable Shape—The Art of Transformation

Not every strike requires an iron fist.
The wisest warriors conquer without lifting a blade—they master the art of control.

Meaning:

Not every battle is won by strength. Some are won by refusing to break.

Hidden Meaning:

The disciplined warrior knows when to strike—
and when to disappear beneath the surface.

Message:

Yielding isn't weakness.
It's strategy.
It's knowing when to absorb instead of resist.
When force fails—flow.
Because not every battle is won by pushing harder.
Some are won by adapting faster.
By bending where others break.
By knowing the difference between retreat and recalibration.
You don't have to fight every wave.
Sometimes, the win is in how you move with it—and rise after.

I. The Illusion of Strength

Warriors are trained to conquer.

To dominate. To bite.

To sharpen every edge until only power remains.

But not every enemy can be crushed.

Some don't fight back—they disappear.

They flow.

They slip through the grip, no matter how tight it clenches.

Water doesn't care how sharp you are.

It cannot be bitten.

It moves.

It adapts.

It survives—

while you bleed from your own teeth.

II. The Warrior Who Cannot Yield Will Break

Trees snap.

Stone cracks.

Steel rusts.

But water remains.

Not because it's harder—

but because it knows when to bend.

The warriors who refuse to yield don't look strong—

they look shattered.

Not by battle—

but by their own refusal to adapt.

Flexibility isn't surrender.
It's survival.
It's precision.
It's power under control.

III. The Misuse of Power

Many mistake power for pressure.
They think control means domination.
They believe the loudest strike always wins.

So they swing wildly.
They burn themselves out.
They try to bite the water.

And the water?
It waits.

Power without discipline is noise.
Power with restraint is command.

IV. Ieyasu Tokugawa Waited While Empires Burned

Born into war in 1543—surrounded by swords, betrayal, and blood.
Tokugawa Ieyasu wasn't the strongest.
He wasn't the loudest.
But he was the last man standing.

While warlords cut each other down for power,
he watched.
He bent where others broke.

He played weak when it kept him alive.
He waited decades—
until timing, not strength, gave him the edge.

He struck once.
And it ended everything.

He unified Japan without screaming.
He ruled for over 250 years without lifting a blade in haste.
Because he knew the truth:
You don't conquer with noise.
You conquer by letting your enemies burn themselves.

"The strong man is not the one who can destroy his enemies.
It is the one who can master himself in their presence."
— *Tokugawa Ieyasu*

He didn't need fire.
He became the calm that outlived it.
Where others snapped —
he endured.

V. The Silent Victory

Victory isn't always violent.
Sometimes, it's still.
Sometimes, it's invisible—
like the warrior who didn't fight...
and still remained.

You cannot bite water.
But water can drown you.
And that's the point.

The undisciplined break themselves.
The disciplined bend—
and rise again.

"Even the sharpest teeth cannot bite water."
— *Silent Threads*

So train your blade—but learn when to sheath it.
Sharpen your edge—but don't rely on it.
Refine your force—but master your restraint.
Because power means nothing if it can't survive the moment it's denied.
Be like water.
Still.
Disciplined.
Unstoppable.
Because in the end,
the ones who last
aren't the loudest.
Or the sharpest.

They're the ones who bent—but never shattered.

SILENT AXIOM VIII

"Our hands can create anything but time."
— *Silent Threads*

The Irreplaceable Blade — The Discipline of Time

Your hands may build everything,
but time builds you.

Meaning:
Time is the only resource that cannot be created, restored, or repeated.

Hidden Meaning:
To waste time isn't passive—it's betrayal.

Message:
Discipline begins with guarding the seconds you'll never get back.

I. The Limit of Creation

There is no tool more powerful than human hands.
They forge swords.
They raise monuments.
They build kingdoms, craft weapons, heal wounds, and break records.

But one thing no hand can shape—is time.

Time doesn't answer to kings.
It can't be stolen.
It can't be rebuilt.
And yet, it's the one thing people burn the fastest.

II. The Subtle Betrayal

Most warriors don't fall in battle—
they fall in delay.

They believe there will always be another day.
Another hour.
Another chance to start.

But time doesn't negotiate.
Every second ignored is gone.
Every delay is self-inflicted decay.

You can rebuild strength.
You can reclaim discipline.
But you will never—

ever—

get those seconds back.

III. The Delusion of the Undisciplined

The undisciplined treat time like it's infinite.
They spend it chasing approval.
Scrolling. Performing. Avoiding.

They confuse movement with progress.
They mistake busyness for purpose.

But the disciplined?
They know time is the most violent resource.

They aim it.
Guard it.
Weaponize it.

Not because they fear time—
but because they respect what it costs.

IV. Nikola Tesla Slept Two Hours to Build Forever

Born in 1856. Obsessed with electricity before the world even understood the spark.
Nikola Tesla didn't have time—he *made* time.

He worked through storms.
Starved for invention.
Slept two hours a night.

While others chased investors, he chased the future.
He wrote blueprints in his mind.
Tested theories with no lab.
Built machines without prototypes—because he believed wasting time on failure was worse than failing itself.

"I do not think you can name many great inventions that have been made by married men."
— *Nikola Tesla*

Translation:
Comfort wastes time.
And he would sacrifice everything—
for one more second with the work.

Tesla died with nothing.
But he gave the world power.
Not just electricity—but the warning:

You don't own time.
You only own what you do with it.

V. The Final Thread
Our hands can create anything—except time.

It cannot be rebuilt.
It cannot be bought.
It cannot be reclaimed.

You will not mourn money.
You will not mourn praise.
You will mourn the time you gave away
for nothing.

So use what remains.
Aim your seconds.

Defend your minutes.
And turn every hour into a weapon.

Because your hands can build kingdoms—
but only time decides who wears the crown.

And time doesn't care who built the throne—only who earned it.

SILENT AXIOM IX

"One must fight darkness until it bleeds light."
— *Silent Threads*

The Warrior's Edge — The Void Is Not Quelled. It Craves the Darkness.

Darkness doesn't leave.
It breaks when you make it bleed.

Meaning:

You cannot negotiate with darkness.
It is only moved by resistance.

Hidden Meaning:

Peace is not given by evil—it is seized from it.

Message:

You don't escape the storm by waiting.
You overcome it by standing inside it.

I. The Reality of Darkness

Darkness does not bargain.
It does not pity.
It does not pause.
It waits for your compromise.
It feeds on hesitation.

It buries those who hope instead of fight.

Peace is not granted.
It is taken.

Those who close their eyes and wait for it to pass
are the first to be consumed.

II. The Warrior's Dilemma

At some point, you will face a darkness that won't leave.
It won't flinch.
It won't respond to your fear—
only your refusal.

You'll be tempted to kneel.
To delay.
To rationalize.

But every compromise is blood in the water.

You cannot avoid what was made to test you.
You cannot escape what you refuse to confront.

III. Bleeding Light from the Darkness

Light is not found.
It is bled.
From scars.
From discipline.
From the nights you refuse to break.

Every act of courage becomes a cut in the dark.
And if you make enough—
it bleeds

IV. Witold Pilecki Entered Hell to Make It Bleed

In 1940, Witold Pilecki did what no soldier had ever done:
He volunteered to be captured and sent to Auschwitz.

Why?
To build a resistance.
To gather proof.
To fight evil from inside the jaws of death.

He watched the darkest cruelty on earth—and took notes.
He smuggled intelligence to the outside world.
He starved, froze, and bled—
but never broke.

After nearly three years, he escaped.
But when the war ended, he was silenced again—
this time by his own country,
for refusing to stop telling the truth.

"I tried to live so that in the hour of my death
I would feel joy rather than fear."
— *Witold Pilecki*

Pilecki didn't just endure darkness—
he exposed it.

And the light that bled from his suffering
still blinds tyrants to this day.

V. Light Demands No Surrender
"One must fight darkness until it bleeds light."
— *Silent Threads*

There is no shortcut.
There is no deal.
There is no peace without pain.

Do not plead.
Do not lower your sword.
Do not look for light—
create it.

Every act of defiance carves a mark.
Every scar becomes a torch.
You don't run from the dark—
you drag it into the light.
And if you hold the line long enough,
even the void must answer to the flame.

SILENT AXIOM X

"Spare no sympathy for self-inflicted wounds."
— *Silent Threads*

A Silent Code—Stand for Pain. Kneel for the Fallen.
Don't beg for mercy from the chains you welded.
Don't kneel for wounds you chose.
You stand.
And you keep standing—until you've earned the right to kneel beside the dead.

Meaning:
Personal accountability is non-negotiable.

Hidden Meaning:
You cannot lead if you're still bleeding from wounds you gave yourself.

Message:
Fix what you broke.
Own what you created.
And bow for no one—unless they died standing.

I. The Wound You Chose

Some pain is dealt by the world.

Some by time.

Some by fate.

But this one?

This one's on you.

You missed the signs.

You ignored the edge.

You chose softness—and now you want sympathy for the blood?

Stand. You don't kneel for a mess you made.

You clean it.

You learn from it.

And you rise.

II. The Architecture of Suffering

Most suffering isn't punishment—it's payment.

A tax on poor choices.

Debt from ignored discipline.

Interest from days you didn't show up.

The undisciplined want a bailout.

They want applause for crawling back.

But warriors know better.

The only mercy for self-inflicted wounds is mastery.

Don't feed the wound.
Don't beg over it.
Stand for the pain. Kneel only for the fallen.

III. The Poison of Justification

The worst kind of lie isn't public—it's private.
The whisper that says,
"It wasn't my fault."

That lie becomes armor.
But armor made of excuses shatters under truth.

Every "I had no choice."
Every "They did this to me."
Every "If only..."

That's not healing.
That's hiding.

And warriors don't hide.
They face. They fix. They stand.

IV. Admiral James Stockdale Refused the Role of Victim

In 1965, U.S. Navy pilot James Stockdale was shot down over Vietnam.
Captured. Tortured. Starved. Broken.

But he was the highest-ranking officer in the Hanoi Hilton—and the only
one who refused to kneel.

They tried to parade him on camera for propaganda.
So he beat his own face with a stool to make himself unusable.

They locked him in solitary for four years.
He led from the shadows—secretly organizing resistance among his fellow POWs.

He admitted his fear.
He admitted his faults.
But never once did he ask to be saved.

And when they offered early release—he refused it.
Because leadership meant staying until they all came home.

"You must never confuse faith that you will prevail in the end... with the discipline to confront the most brutal facts of your current reality."
— James Stockdale

He didn't cry for sympathy.
He didn't play the victim.
He endured. Led. And bled quietly—so others could survive.

V. The Warrior Who Leads Through Pain

Leadership doesn't begin with power.
It begins with pain—and the decision to take ownership of it.

You will find broken bridges you set fire to.
You'll uncover scars you've kept hidden behind excuses.
You'll find wreckage you once blamed on fate—that you caused.

Good.

Now fix it.
Don't run from the damage.
Don't decorate it with regret.
Don't kneel at the altar of your own weakness.

Stand.
Not for pride.
Not for pity.
But because no one follows a man
still begging for mercy
from the wounds he gave himself.

Pain isn't your disqualifier—
it's your initiation.

You want to lead?
Then stop asking for mercy from the cage you built—
and start becoming the man who never needed saving.

CHAPTER CLOSING: WHERE SCARS BECOME SALVATION

The pain didn't break you. It built you.

There are battles only you can fight—not with armies, not with applause, but in silence, in sweat, and in scars. These are the wars between who you were and who you refuse to remain.

You've faced the first enemy: yourself—the version that traded purpose for pity, that knew better and still stayed soft, that called comfort "peace" when it was really decay. But warriors don't beg. They don't explain. They evolve.

You've stopped chasing revenge from others and started forging it from within. You don't just fight darkness—you make it bleed. Because you understand now: light doesn't arrive—it's carved.

You've learned that not every battle can be won by brute force, that even sharp teeth can't bite water, that control isn't domination—it's discipline. You've learned that leadership isn't solitary. The lone wolf dies. The pack survives.

You've learned that pain isn't waiting to be healed—it's waiting to be harnessed.

Not to be pitied.

To be **aimed**.

Because some scars don't fade.

They sharpen.

They mark the places where weakness was buried

and something harder took its place.
You don't owe the world an explanation.
Just proof you didn't need saving.

I. Admiral James Stockdale — The Chain Didn't Break Him

He was born in 1923, in Abingdon, Illinois—a farm town built on grit and silence.
Son of a midwestern educator.
Student of philosophy, of Epictetus, of the Stoics.
Trained as a naval aviator.
Hardened in the cockpit.
Sharpened in thought before war ever touched his flesh.

He didn't just fly—he studied the battlefield like a scholar of suffering.
And when Vietnam took him down, he didn't plead for mercy—he became a weapon of will.

Shot down. Captured. Tortured.
Seven years in the Hanoi Hilton.
Beaten until bones snapped.
Held in darkness.
Mocked, broken, starved.
But never surrendered.

They offered him early release.
He refused.
Because his men came first.

"You must never confuse faith that you will prevail in the end...
with the discipline to confront the brutal facts of your current reality."
— Admiral James Stockdale

He didn't ask for comfort.
He embraced the truth: brutal, bare, and honest.
And in doing so, he proved the highest form of leadership isn't strategy—
it's presence.

He didn't leave the prison the same man.
He left it forged—and that silence followed him forever.

II. David Goggins — The Man Who Broke His Own Chains

He was born in 1975, in Buffalo, New York—into chaos.
Into abuse.
Into silence that hurt more than the noise.

Son of violence.
Student of failure.
Outcast in his own body—obese, ashamed, unnoticed.

He wasn't raised by warriors.
He was raised by fear.
But inside that fear, a voice refused to die.

He watched his father beat his mother.
He learned early: pain doesn't go away—you either break from it, or
build through it.

And Goggins?
He built.

"You are in danger of living a life so comfortable and soft,
that you will die without ever realizing your true potential."
— *David Goggins*

He didn't stumble into greatness.
He crawled into it—bleeding, blind, and alone.

Failed ASVAB.
Bullied.
Mocked.
Obese at 300+ pounds.

But he lost the weight.
Lost the lies.
And found the edge no one else would walk.

He became a Navy SEAL.
A fire-breather.
A living myth.

Three Hell Weeks.
Ultramarathons.
Pain rituals that would break gods.

His silence wasn't fear.
It was war.

Every scar became his armor.
Every mile became proof.

Every chain he once wore, he melted down and reforged into a blade.

Goggins didn't escape hell.
He ran into it—and built a throne.

III. Final Reflection — The Discipline to Outlive the Wound

Stockdale survived seven years of chains—because he refused to kneel to false hope.
Goggins built his own chains—then shattered them with the edge of his discipline.

Neither of them ran from pain.
They ran into it.
Through it.
Past it.

That's what you've become now.
Not someone who dodges the blow—someone who stands for it.
Bleeds.
And leads forward.

You don't wear wounds like decoration.
You wear them like truth.
Earned. Forged. Carried.

This chapter didn't teach you to feel better.
It taught you how to *be* better.
It made you responsible for your evolution.

And now?
You don't run.
You don't beg.
You don't bow.

You lead—through the storm, through the silence, through the pain.
Because the wound no longer owns you.

The Final Creed
Stand for the pain.
Kneel for the fallen.
Lead forward.

Because warriors don't ask for mercy—
they break the chain
and carry the weight
until someone else can stand again.

Chains break when discipline sharpens silence into action.

3

THE SURVIVOR'S CODE

You weren't chosen to survive.
You were built to endure.

There is a difference between surviving and living. The world is full of survivors—empty, hollow, still breathing—but already gone. Existing is easy. Enduring is another matter entirely.

This chapter is not about breathing air. It is about holding your ground when the world caves in. It is about learning the truth most won't say aloud: survival is not a gift. It is a war.

The storms come. The undisciplined fold. The darkness lingers. They collapse. They whisper to themselves, "It's enough just to survive."

No—it's not.

The survivor does not simply suffer. The survivor learns to stand inside the suffering. Pain isn't the threat—it's the teacher. Fear isn't the end—it's the threshold. Those who collapse at the first taste of loss never belonged to the fight. The ones who endure? They learned, step by step, blow by blow, how to make survival the blade no one saw coming.

Survival is not passive. It is not waiting. It is not hoping. It is discipline—earned, sharpened, reforged every time you refuse to stay down.

This is what separates the warrior from the victim. Not the strength to win every battle—but the refusal to stay broken, even when losing feels easier.

This is the code passed between those who have bled, and those who will. It is not carved into stone. It is etched into scars, burned into callouses, and held in silence by those who have nothing left—except the will to endure.

The world will strip you bare. It will rob you. It will leave you alone. And it will dare you to stand.

The Survivor's Code is not a list of rules—it is a reminder. You will suffer. You will be outnumbered. You will want to quit. And when you do? The code will decide whether you crawl or rise.

This is not for those looking for a shortcut. This is for those ready to stand—even if they stand alone.

SILENT AXIOM XI

"It's not death I'm chasing—I'm simply trying to survive your way of life."
— *Silent Threads*

The Survivor's Creed—Refuse the Quiet Grave

You're not afraid to die.
You're afraid to disappear while still alive.

Meaning:
Many are not afraid of death—but of living a life dictated by others.

Hidden Meaning:
Society can be more lethal than mortality. It kills you slowly with expectations you never agreed to.

Message:
Survival is resisting conformity.
To live freely, you must outlast more than time—you must outlast their expectations.

I. The False Fear of Death

Most don't fear death.
They fear dying as someone they never chose to be.
A life dictated.
A fire buried.
A legacy traded for likes.

Warriors don't run from death—
they run from becoming someone else's shadow.

This isn't about recklessness.
It's about refusal—
to surrender your identity for acceptance.

Because there's a worse fate than death—
a life unlived.

II. Society as the Silent Killer

The most dangerous killer doesn't wear armor.
It wears comfort.
It offers praise for obedience.
It rewards softness with silence—
and calls it peace.

"Be quiet."
"Be normal."
"Fit in."

Conformity is a drug.
And most overdose quietly—

buried under a life they never wanted.

The warrior survives war.
But the rarest ones?
Survive society.

III. The Hidden Death

There's a kind of death no one speaks of.
It doesn't bleed.
Doesn't leave scars.
But it erases you just the same.

It's the death of self.
The slow erasure of your fire
for a seat at the table of people who never earned your silence.

You trade pieces of who you are
until one day you look in the mirror—
and see nothing that resembles truth.

No tombstone.
No funeral.
Just a slow, silent erasure—
and a fire no one remembered to mourn.

IV. Boudica Burned the Empire That Betrayed Her

She was born into warrior blood—queen of the Iceni tribe in first century Britannia.
A mother. A leader. A woman Rome thought it could tame.

When her husband died, the Romans stole her land, flogged her, and raped her daughters—
a message meant to silence her.

But Boudica didn't break.
She rose.

With no title recognized by Rome, no crown on her head,
she led an uprising that burned Roman cities to the ground.

London. Colchester. Verulamium.
Over 70,000 dead—not out of vengeance...
but to remind the world what happens when you try to erase a warrior.

"I am not fighting for my kingdom and wealth.
I am fighting as an ordinary person for my lost freedom, my bruised body,
and the outraged chastity of my daughters."
— Boudica, according to Tacitus

She didn't ask for a seat at Rome's table.
She flipped the table.

She didn't survive by playing their game.
She survived by refusing to kneel to it.

Even in defeat, her fire became myth.

Her name became rebellion.

And her silence became a war cry that still echoes through history.

V. The Survivor's Creed

You will be told to tone it down.

To shrink.

To accept their version of success.

To sit at the table and eat what they hand you.

They will dress it up as wisdom.

But it's submission.

Don't take their food.

Burn their table.

Build your own.

You're not chasing death.

You're running from a life designed to erase you.

So don't shrink.

Don't wait to be seen.

Because the real fear?

Isn't dying.

It's disappearing while still alive.

SILENT AXIOM XII

"I didn't build the bridge for my enemies to succeed—I built it to learn from their mistakes."
— *Silent Threads*

The Watcher's Edge—When Stillness Becomes the Strategy

Patience isn't surrender.
It's surveillance.

Meaning:
Failure is a better teacher than victory.

Hidden Meaning:
You gain more by observing enemies than fighting them.

Message:
Study, adapt, and grow—even when outnumbered.

I. Why Build the Bridge?

Not every bridge is built for peace.
Some are built for patience.

The untrained panic at the sight of enemies crossing—
thinking they've already lost.
They believe every move forward by an opponent is their own failure.

But the wise know:
The bridge is not for them—it's for you.

It's bait.
It's a vantage point.
It's a lesson waiting to be given.

I didn't build the bridge for my enemies to win—
I built it so I could stand still, watch, and learn.

II. The Lessons They Carry

The mistake is thinking you need to stop every opponent.
You don't.

Most enemies expose themselves—
not with weapons,
but with performance.
Loud moves. Desperate signals.
Pride pretending to be power.
Fear dressed as fury.

Let them cross the bridge.
Watch them carry the weight they thought was yours.

If you rush to block the way, you'll miss the show.
You'll miss what they hand you—
the blueprint to their weakness.

There is no teacher like watching someone fail
under the weight of their own assumptions.

III. The Advantage of Stillness

Outnumbered?
Good.
It forces you to be smarter.

Outmatched?
Maybe—but they're the ones marching blindly, not you.

The disciplined don't fight first—they watch.
They study every footstep, every decision, every flaw.

They let their enemies teach them—in real time.

The world loves to reward noise.
But noise is just the sound of strategy dying.

Stay still long enough—
and the undisciplined will reveal their hand.

IV. Why You Don't Burn the Bridge

It's tempting to light it up.
To destroy it before they reach you.

But destroy the bridge too soon—
and you destroy the opportunity.

You'll never know what could have been learned.

Fools panic and burn.
The patient observe and adapt.

You don't build bridges to stop the enemy—
you build them to study.

Let them cross.
Let them move.
Let them stumble.

V. The Closing Thread
You don't build for them.
You build for you.

A bridge is just a stage.
An enemy is just an unwitting teacher.

When you're outnumbered, when you're outgunned—
be still.
Be patient.

And when their mistakes are paid in full—
walk the bridge you built to bury them.

SILENT AXIOM XIII

"Do not allow victory to become your defeat—success has no limits."
— *Silent Threads*

The Discipline of Aftermath —
When Winning Becomes the Trap
Victory isn't the finish line.
It's the trigger for the next war.

Meaning:
Success can seduce you into stagnation.

Hidden Meaning:
Many lose after they win because they stop growing.

Message:
Success is not the finish line; it is the next starting point.

I. The Trap of Victory
Victory is praised, envied, and desired—
but it is also a snare.

The moment you taste it, it whispers:
"You've made it. Rest."

That is how most are defeated—
not by enemies,
but by their own success.

Success tempts warriors into laying down their weapons too soon.
It tells you the work is finished.
The mountain is climbed.
The crown is earned.

But the disciplined know better.
There is no finish line.
There is only the next fight.

II. The Danger of Stagnation

The most dangerous opponent isn't the enemy you see—
it's the comfort you feel after winning.

Comfort makes you slow.
It dulls your edge.
It turns the hunter into the hunted.

Warriors don't lose because they are weak—
they lose because they thought winning meant they could stop moving.

Growth does not end at success—
success is simply the checkpoint.

The ones who survive?
They are the ones who step off the podium
and go straight back to sharpening the blade.

III. Success Is Not Safety

There is no safety in success.
It is a temporary reward, not a permanent shelter.

The disciplined know that winning today
does not protect you tomorrow.

It's the ones who cling to yesterday's victory who fall hardest.

Success is not proof that you're finished—
it's proof that you were capable.
But capability expires if you don't maintain it.

The disciplined understand:
the same grind that built you is the only thing that will keep you.

IV. The Endless Ascent

There is no summit.
There is no crown that cannot rust.
There is no victory that cannot fade.

The warrior does not celebrate forever—
they reset.
They refocus.
They climb again.

Victory is a signal, not a stopping point.
It says:
"You are ready for more."

But only the disciplined will hear it.

V. The Closing Thread

Success is a sedative—
and most overdoses happen after the applause.

Do not confuse the reward with the mission.
Do not crown yourself for surviving one storm
when the sky is still black.

You were built to outlast the win—
because the next war is already watching.

Reset the edge.
Reload the focus.
Then move without noise—like the win never happened.

**Because real warriors don't chase crowns—
they outlast thrones.**

SILENT AXIOM XIV

"The greatest opportunities are forged from the ashes of compromise."
— *Silent Threads*

The Ashes We Build With —
When Pride Becomes the Prison

Greatness doesn't rise from stubbornness—
it rises from what survives the fire.

Meaning:

True strength isn't about refusing to bend—it's about knowing *when* to.
Pride disguised as conviction will burn your chances, your allies, and
your legacy.
What remains after that fire—that's what you were supposed to build with.

Hidden Meaning:

We're taught to never back down.
But sometimes "holding the line" is just a performance of ego.
You're not standing tall—you're standing *alone*.
And the ash beneath your feet?
It wasn't fate. It wasn't betrayal.
It was **you**, choosing pride over progress.
Compromise isn't surrender—it's strategy.
It's the heat that melts arrogance into **adaptability**.

Message / Takeaway:
You don't lose the war because you bent.
You lose because you *refused to bend when it mattered.*
Opportunities come not from domination—but collaboration.
Let pride die. Let ego burn.
Because what you forge from those ashes?
That's your second chance.
That's the edge your enemies didn't see coming.

I. The Cost of Pride
Pride will make you deaf.
It will make you blind.
It will convince you that stubbornness is strength—
and by the time you realize the truth,
you'll be standing in the ashes of what could have been.

Most warriors lose not because they lacked power—
but because they refused to listen.
Refused to bend.
Refused to share the load.

You think you're holding the line—
but you're just holding yourself back.

II. Ashes Are Self-Inflicted

Those ashes?
They didn't fall from the sky.
You lit the match.
You fed the fire.
You burned the bridge.

How many alliances died
because one warrior refused to compromise?

How many victories slipped away
because you needed to be right
more than you needed to win?

The ashes beneath your feet
are not failure.
They are ego—
burned to dust.

III. The Furnace of Compromise

But here's the truth:
ashes aren't just ruin—
they are fuel.

It is only after the pride burns away
that you can forge something real.
Something stronger.
Something that won't collapse under pressure.

Compromise isn't weakness.
It's discipline.
It's knowing when to lock shields instead of swords.

The lone wolf dies.
The pack survives.
Simple.

Because knowing when to bend isn't surrender—
it's the strategy that keeps the blade from breaking.

IV. The Unseen Edge

Those too proud to bend will break.
Those too blind to compromise will fade.

But the disciplined?
They use the ashes.
They build.
They adapt.

They find opportunity
where the stubborn only find loss.

What you couldn't see through arrogance—
you'll see clearly once the smoke clears.

V. The Final Thread
"The greatest opportunities are forged from the ashes of compromise."
— *Silent Threads*

Not every battle is won by force.
Not every stand needs to be alone.

Let the pride burn.
Let the ego fall.

And when it does—
pick up the ashes,
shape a legacy no flame can touch,
and rise as something they can't erase.

SILENT AXIOM XV

"In the shadow of a hero, a coward endures."
— *Silent Threads*

The Coward with a Crown — In the Shadows, They Feed on Your Reign

They don't follow your lead—
they survive behind your legacy.

Meaning:
Not everyone beside you is a warrior—some just hide behind one.

Hidden Meaning:
Loyalty is often a disguise for survival.

Message:
Proximity is not courage—it's often just the coward's hiding place.

I. Shadows Are Deceiving

Every warrior will eventually look around and see others standing close.
Side by side. Shoulder to shoulder.

But proximity does not equal loyalty.
It does not equal courage.

Some stand beside you because they are strong.
Some stand beside you because they have nowhere else to go.
And some?
They stand beside you because your shadow hides their fear.

Cowards endure when they're shielded by someone else's courage.
Not every ally is an ally.

II. The Mask of Loyalty

Cowards don't always run.
Some cling tight.

They hide behind the bold.
They speak when it's safe.
They swear loyalty under the banner of your strength.

But the moment the ground shakes,
the moment the walls close in,
the moment they are alone—
they are gone.

This is not betrayal.
It is exposure.

When the fire comes,
the mask melts.
And what remains is the truth—
they were never warriors.
Just shadows wearing your colors.

III. Actions, Not Appearances

You don't judge men by how close they stand when the battle is easy.
You judge them by how they stand when the storm breaks.

Watch them when no one is watching.
Watch them when things fall apart.
Watch them when their name isn't being called.

That's where courage shows itself.
Or where cowardice takes over.

Silence reveals more than noise.
And proximity means nothing if the hands beside you won't lift when it counts.

IV. The Weight of Endurance

Endurance is not about simply standing there.
It's about holding the line when everything screams to retreat.

The hero holds.
The coward endures—quietly hoping someone else will do the work.

And yet,
it is the coward's endurance—not courage—
that will weigh you down when the real fight arrives.

Because when you expect them to fight—
they will only freeze,
or worse—run.

V. The Closing Thread
"In the shadow of a hero, a coward endures."
— *Silent Threads*

And when the trial comes,
the shadow fades.

Survival is not just living.
It is defying the collapse of self.

These codes—
they are not suggestions.
They are not guidelines.
They are vital.

Because when the moment comes,
you won't have time to check who's standing next to you.
Titles disappear. Applause dies. And the truth steps forward.
And you'll already know—
by whether or not you feel them lift the weight.

CHAPTER CLOSING: THE SILENT WARS

The throne was never empty—you just weren't listening.

Not all survival is physical. Some battles are fought at tables, behind doors, or beneath the crushing weight of responsibility.

The survivor is not always the bloodied soldier—sometimes it is the leader who stands alone when the world demands they break.

Not all endurance is on the battlefield. Sometimes it is in compromise. Sometimes it is in watching the bridges you built collapse, and still choosing to rebuild them, better than before.

The loud will always be remembered first—but it is the quiet who are remembered longest.

The ones who didn't chase applause but kept showing up after the cheers died down. The ones who didn't fall apart after the betrayal, but gathered the pieces and made something unshakable. Survival isn't about being untouched. It's about what you do after the damage is done. It's about rising without an audience. It's about suffering with your mouth shut—and still showing up with your hands ready.

There will be days when your name is praised, and nights when it's dragged through the dirt. Neither defines you.

Your legacy isn't built in your best moment—it's built in your worst.

The moments when you felt betrayal, felt loneliness, felt the weight of everything you swore to carry—and you carried it anyway.

No crown is earned without cost. No victory is clean. No discipline is forged without first being fractured.

You don't rise by luck. You rise because you refuse to fall for long.

And the next time the world tries to count you out—stay silent.

Let them forget you. Let them think the throne is unguarded. Let them believe your silence means surrender.

And when they step forward to claim what was never theirs—make your move.

One strike. No warning. Nothing left to prove.

Because you didn't survive to be seen—You survived to reign.

I. Abraham Lincoln — The Reluctant Warrior of Compromise

Lincoln did not set out to burn bridges—he tried to preserve them.

He tried compromise.

He tried peace.

But some wars are unavoidable.

When compromise failed, and the nation tore itself apart, Lincoln stood inside the ashes—and forged something greater.

The United States was not preserved through smooth negotiations.

It was reforged through sacrifice and steel.

Famous Quote:

"The dogmas of the quiet past are inadequate to the stormy present."
— Abraham Lincoln, Annual Message to Congress, December 1, 1862

Lincoln didn't worship conflict—he hated it.

But he understood the code:

Some things must burn before they can be rebuilt.

The Civil War was not just a clash of armies—it was the death of compromise and the birth of a new nation, forged from the ashes.

II. Marcus Aurelius—The Stoic Who Saw Through Cowards

Marcus Aurelius wore the purple of Rome, but walked like a soldier. He ruled an empire surrounded by those who bowed easily, praised him publicly, but trembled privately.

He understood what most never will: not every man beside you shares your courage.

Famous Quote:
"Waste no more time arguing about what a good man should be. Be one."
— *Marcus Aurelius*, Meditations, *Book 10.16*

Cowards stood in his shadow, hiding behind the shield of the Emperor, hoping they'd never be called forward.

Marcus endured not just enemies at the empire's borders, but false allies at his table.

He wrote not for others, but to himself—reminding himself daily that only actions reveal the real warriors.

Beyond the Shadows
The throne isn't found in the light—it's claimed in the dark.

This is the survivor's burden—to walk with those who may never fight beside you, to speak knowing most will only nod without understanding, and to endure—not just the obvious enemies—, but the quiet disappointments of those you once trusted.

The Survivor's Code was never about looking the part—it is about living the part.

Survival is not just scraping through the storm.

It is standing afterward, without apology, without compromise, and without illusion.

The weak may walk in your shadow.

Let them.

But make sure that when the real fight comes, you are the one still standing.

4

HIDDEN CAGES

*There is no prison more effective
than the one you build yourself.*

Not all cages are made of steel. Not all locks need keys. Some are softer. Some wear the mask of comfort. Others wear the crown of success. But no matter how polished or padded, they trap you just the same.

This chapter isn't about avoiding obvious danger. It's about recognizing the hidden traps you invited into your life. The ones you labeled as normal. The ones you called stability. The ones you convinced yourself were earned. But underneath? They were chains. And worse—you forged them.

No one handed you this cage. You built it. Slowly. Silently. One compromise at a time. One excuse at a time. One quiet surrender at a time. You didn't think you were quitting—you thought you were adapting. Surviving. Playing it smart. But in reality, you were surrendering in slow motion.

You mistook routine for peace. You told yourself comfort was a reward. You convinced yourself that stillness was strategy—when in truth, it was stagnation. And now? You're still breathing. Still showing up. But nothing inside you burns. Nothing sharpens. Nothing rises.

Hidden cages don't stop your heartbeat—they silence your fire. They don't scream. They whisper. They convince you that what you have is enough. They tell you your ambition is foolish. They shrink your dreams. They dull your edge. And then one day, you wake up and realize: you've been loyal to a version of yourself you outgrew years ago.

This chapter isn't about escape. It's about demolition. It's about hunting down every soft link you welded in silence—and melting it. One by one. Until your edge returns.

You don't break free by waiting for rescue. You break free by owning the truth. You look yourself in the mirror and say:

"I built this cage. Now I'm going to burn it down."

Every title you've hidden behind. Every excuse you framed as logic. Every comfort you mistook for purpose. Every lie you told yourself to avoid discomfort. It all goes in the fire.

Because comfort isn't peace. Success isn't safety. And survival? It was never the goal.

Reign is.

This isn't a motivational speech. This is a confrontation—between the version of you that settled and the version of you that's still buried under the weight of potential.

If you're tired, good. If you're angry, even better. That tension you feel right now? That's the cage starting to rattle. That's the old you sensing its end. And it *should* end—because you weren't born to decorate your cage. You were built to destroy it.

So light the match. Shatter the locks. And walk through the fire wearing every scar like armor.

The world doesn't need another prisoner pretending to be strong.

It needs warriors who remember exactly how the cage was built—and still choose to burn it down.

This chapter wasn't written from theory—it was pulled from the fire of a man who lived it.

Eric Kilcullen didn't borrow these lessons—he bled for them. The discipline, the confrontation, the refusal to settle—it wasn't built on comfort. It was forged from silence. From betrayal. From rising after self-inflicted collapse, and still choosing to lead.

He's not a speaker trying to be profound—he's a survivor who became a strategist. A warrior who learned that presence doesn't require noise. That leadership begins with owning your wreckage. That reign isn't granted—it's reclaimed, scar by scar.

He didn't just burn his past. He turned it into armor.

He made the fire kneel.

And now it's your turn.

Not just to escape—but to rise so far beyond the cage,

that it begs for the sound of your chains

Welcome to the next war.

You're not locked in. You're being called out.

SILENT AXIOM XVI

"Success bows to three forces—
Education, Experience, and Exposure."
— *Silent Threads*

The Depth That Holds

Surface wins can't carry the weight. Only depth can.

Meaning:

Success doesn't show up because you want it. It doesn't respond to noise or luck. It yields only to those who've earned the right to carry it—and that right is forged through three forces:

Education (what you didn't know),

Experience (what you couldn't control),

Exposure (what you've never seen).

You cannot cheat these. You can only engage them—or be broken by them later.

Hidden Meaning:

The ones who endure aren't always the fastest or the loudest—they're the ones who went deeper. They studied when no one asked them to. They suffered where others avoided pain. They stepped into difference, discomfort, and the unknown. These are the people with substance, not just momentum. They don't flinch under pressure, because they've bled through worse. They don't crack under scrutiny, because they've lived what others only memorize.

Message:
You can fake the look—for a while.
You can chase attention—and still lose yourself.
You can grab quick wins—and still crumble when tested.

Because success doesn't care how loud you were.
It cares how deep you went.

I. The First Force: Education

Education is not about credentials.
It's about comprehension.
It's the quiet pursuit of truth—
the skill of asking sharper questions.

It builds your framework—
so when the test comes,
you don't guess.
You move with precision.

Most stop learning once they're told they've arrived.
But the strong never stop.
They read.
They refine.
They remain students of the mission.

Education isn't just school.
It's study.
It's observation.
It's humility.
It's saying, "I don't know—yet."

And building from there.

II. The Second Force: Experience

There are lessons you can only learn by bleeding.
Failure teaches what theory can't.
Loss teaches what success never will.
Survival teaches what planning couldn't.

Experience gives your words weight.
It gives your instincts shape.
It forges the line between confidence and competence.

The ones who haven't suffered may sound brilliant—
until something goes wrong.

Then the ones with scars take control.
Not because they're louder—
but because they've been there before.
And they don't flinch.

III. The Third Force: Exposure

You can't evolve if you never leave your echo chamber.
You need tension.
You need difference.
You need disruption.

You need to sit across from people
Who think differently.
Live differently.

Challenge your lens.

Exposure breaks the illusion
That your way is the only way.
It doesn't dilute conviction—
it sharpens clarity.

Leaders who haven't been exposed to real diversity—
collapse under nuance.
But the exposed?
They adapt.
Not by compromise.
But by seeing the full board.

IV. Shortcut Nothing

You can win fast—but you won't last.
You can go viral—but you won't matter.
You can look the part—but fold under pressure.

If you haven't earned your voice through depth,
it will fail when the pressure comes.

The world will ask:
- Have you learned enough?
- Have you lived enough?
- Have you seen enough?

If the answer is, "No"—
then success won't bow.
It'll break you instead.

Ask Kimberly "Kym" Hodges.
She's not on magazine covers.
She doesn't brag in soundbites.

But in shadows—where warriors are built—her name echoes.
Former Army Intelligence.
Trained in counterterrorism.
Fluent in pressure, fluent in pain, fluent in silence.

She's walked through warzones across continents,
tot for glory—
but to forge others who'd survive when no one's watching.

"If you bleed in training, you won't in combat."
— Kimberly "Kym" Hodges

She didn't say it to go viral.
Others said it *because she earned it.*

She shortcut nothing.
And now?
Her legacy bleeds into the next warrior who doesn't flinch.

V. The Depth That Holds
"Success bows to three forces—Education, Experience, and Exposure."
— *Silent Threads*

The ones who last
aren't the ones who got there first—
they're the ones who built what couldn't be broken.

They studied more.
Endured more.
Stepped further.
And in doing so—
they became undeniable.

Shortcut nothing.
Chase everything worth earning.
And when success finally arrives,
it won't ask how loud you were.
It'll ask how deep you went—
and whether you were ready to hold it.

SILENT AXIOM XVII

"Confusing volume for weight is how the weak mistake the strong."
— *Silent Threads*

The Weight That Doesn't Flinch

Power doesn't ask to be heard. It asks to be carried.

Meaning:

The world often rewards the loudest voice in the room—not the wisest, not the strongest. Volume grabs attention, but it doesn't prove capability. In moments of fear, emptiness, or insecurity, noise is mistaken for power. But real power doesn't scream for attention. It speaks through presence, action, and consequence.

Hidden Meaning:

True strength doesn't need to be seen. It doesn't chase applause or validation. It doesn't announce its arrival or demand space—it simply claims it. Quiet strength doesn't need the spotlight, because it owns it without asking. The strongest people in the room are often the least vocal because they have nothing to prove. Their energy is louder than any words.

Message:

Don't mistake spectacle for strength. Don't let noise distract you from truth. Substance is almost never loud. The more someone needs you to hear them, the less likely they are to carry the weight when it matters. Learn to separate signal from sound. Trust your instincts to follow weight—not volume.

I. The Illusion of Noise

There are those who believe the louder they shout, the truer their words become.

They flood the room with sound, hoping it will cover the cracks in their argument.

But repetition isn't truth.

And volume isn't power.

It's performance.

It's panic.

It's the sound of someone hoping you won't look too closely.

Because when you strip away the noise, there's often nothing underneath.

Real strength doesn't rush to be heard.

It doesn't panic when challenged.

It doesn't fight for attention—it earns it through action.

It knows the difference between being noticed and being felt.

Noise wins the moment

but weight wins the war.

II. The Weight That Doesn't Flinch

True strength doesn't twitch or fidget.

It doesn't react to every sound in the room.

It *holds*.

It *waits*.

It *measures*.

The strongest hands aren't the ones clenched in anger—

they're the ones holding the line when everything else shakes.

Real strength doesn't need to speak loudly.
Its presence is already understood.
It doesn't rise with approval.
It moves with purpose.
When everything else fractures—
the one who remains steady has already won.

III. Watch the Work, Not the Volume

Don't judge strength by who talks the most.
Judge it by who moves when no one is watching.

The loudest in the room may draw your attention—
but they rarely carry responsibility.

Watch who works when the crowd is gone.
Watch who stays when the applause fades.
Watch who still lifts when the praise is over.
That's where strength lives.

Substance is found in the work done without recognition.
It's in the actions that don't need to be validated.
That's where truth hides—
and that's where real warriors leave their mark.

IV. Anchors over Echoes

Some need the spotlight to function.
They only act when the lights are on them.

But when the fire comes—
when it's time for the real test—
the loud will falter.
They'll retreat into the crowd they once stood above.

Their strength was never theirs to begin with.
It was borrowed—from the applause, from the noise.

But real trials aren't fought in crowds.
They're fought in silence.
In isolation.
No lights.
No cheers.

And when that moment arrives—
you'll see who was built to last,
and who was simply elevated by attention.
The loud will scatter.
The quiet will stand.

"Excellence means when a man or woman asks of himself more than
others do."
— José Ortega y Gasset

That's the difference.
The quiet don't wait to be tested—they train without witness.
They don't rise because they were watched.

They rise because they held themselves to a higher standard
long before the world expected it from them.

V. The Weight That Remains
"Confusing volume for weight is how the weak mistake the strong."
— *Silent Threads*

When the fire comes,
it won't ask who shouted the loudest.
It will ask who stayed standing.
Who lifted more than their share.
Who showed up when the crowd was gone —
and the work was heavy.

The crowd will move on.
The noise will collapse.
The praise will fade.

But the ones who held the line?
Their strength will still be there.
Not echoing.
Not pleading for recognition —
just present.

Final Strike

Real weight doesn't vanish.
It settles in the bones—it anchors.
Etched into the warriors who withstood its wrath.

SILENT AXIOM XVIII

"To quench a shark's thirst—feed it blood."
— *Silent Threads*

The Maw Beneath the Surface

Some hungers don't fade.
They must be fed—or mastered.

Meaning:

Drive. Rage. Ambition. Vengeance.
These aren't flaws—they're forces.
Ignore them, and they rise at the wrong time.
Understand them—and they become weapons.

Hidden Meaning:

A shark lives in water, yet thirsts for blood.
It doesn't sip its surroundings—it hunts what disrupts them.

Likewise, what moves you isn't peace—it's pressure.
The ones who break aren't monsters—
they're the ones who pretended they didn't have one.

You can't tame what you won't name.
But you *can* train it.
That's the difference between liability and legacy.

Message:
Stop apologizing for your hunger.
Don't bury your darkness—build with it.

Shape it. Sharpen it. Aim it.
The ones who last didn't silence the beast—
they gave it orders.

I. The Predator Evolves

You weren't made for passivity.
You weren't built only for calm.

There's something inside you that doesn't crave peace—it craves proof.
Don't sedate it. Don't fake "fine."

Study it. Train it. Control it.

The world says:
"Be polite. Shrink. Fit in."

But beneath that?
A pulse. A hunger. A question.

Not to destroy—to dominate.
Not to harm—to carve.
Not to survive—to evolve.

That's not shameful.
That's your edge.

But an edge without discipline becomes a wound.

So sharpen with silence.
Move with meaning.

A predator that evolves doesn't chase—
it reigns.

Balance strength with wisdom.
Forge power with purpose.

II. The Danger of Denial

What you suppress, you weaponize—by accident.

Ignore the wolf, and it breaks through the wall.
Deny your rage—it festers.
Deny your instincts—they break out untrained.

People don't snap because they're evil.
They snap because they've been *caging chaos* for too long.

Stillness isn't weakness.
It's the monster—catching its breath.

III. Feeding Without Falling

Feeding the shark doesn't mean letting it thrash.
It means giving it target.

You don't unleash the wolf on civilians—

you point it at the mountain.
You give it the weight no one else can carry.

That hunger in you?
It's not a defect.
It's drive.

But unshaped?
It becomes destruction.

Feed it purpose.
Feed it hardship.
Feed it a mission worthy of its heat.

Then release it.

IV. The Warrior's Calibration
From Fist to Blade of Precision

"Discipline is doing what you hate to do, but doing it like you love it."
— *Mike Tyson*

Tyson is the paradox:
a storm who learned to walk in silence.

He didn't kill the shark inside—he trained it.
He speaks softly now—because he's roared loudly before.
He doesn't swing first—he calculates.

This isn't weakness.
It's reign.
It's what mastery looks like after war.

**"I'm the most brutal and ruthless conqueror...
but I'm trying to change my life."**
— Mike Tyson

V. Master the Maw

You don't silence the predator—you name it.
You don't bury the instinct—you build around it.

That's why elite warriors train under pressure.
Because tension isn't the enemy.
It's the proving ground.

Rage untrained is reckless.
Rage calibrated is strategy.

The ones who endure?
Aren't calm by nature.
They're cold—by confrontation.

They don't pretend they're tame.
They've simply trained the threat.

They didn't run from the hunger—
they aimed it.
And mastered the maw.

Monster Theory: The Creed

To feed a monster—you must think like one.
To lead it—you must *become* one.

Sharks don't ask permission.
They don't sip still water—they hunt what bleeds.
They don't wait for calm—they strike in current.

You weren't born to float.
You were built to cut through storm.

Become cold.
Become clear.
And when the pressure rises—

let them meet the part of you
that trained in silence,
sharpened in shadows,
and never once needed applause.

SILENT AXIOM XIX

"Hate becomes your reign."
— *Silent Threads*

The Throne They Built for You
They didn't stop you.
They crowned you—in spite of themselves.

Meaning:
Hate is energy. And energy can be converted.
It's not just resistance; it's recognition.
They don't attack what doesn't matter.
So when they hate—don't retreat.
Advance.

Hidden Meaning:
They hated your presence—because it disrupted their comfort.
They feared your rise—because it exposed their weakness.

Hate is proof you're visible.
And if you master it—
it becomes your crown.

Message:
Don't flinch.
Don't fold.
Don't beg.

Let their hate build your throne.
Turn rejection into resolve.

And remember:
the loudest hate is just the echo of a throne being built.
They won't hand you the crown—
they'll forge it trying to take you down.

I. Crowned by Opposition

Most chase applause.
You got backlash. Criticism. Doubt. Rejection.

Perfect.

Because every ounce of their hate was a map—
Pointing to where you were already winning.

They hated what they couldn't dismiss.
What they couldn't become.
What they could no longer ignore.

Good.

Because now you know:
you're already on the throne.

II. Weaponize the Venom

You have two choices:
absorb it and break.
Or absorb it and burn hotter.

Hate is pressure—
but pressure makes blades.

Take it all:
Every whisper.
Every jab.
Every attempt to erase you.

And use it.
Let it sharpen you.
Let it remind you:
if they're hating—you're still rising.

III. Seen, Whether They Admit It or Not

They won't speak your name—but they're watching.
They'll act like you don't matter—but mimic your moves in silence.

Let them.
Keep building.

Their silence is just envy in disguise.
And the longer you rise,
the more their hate begins to sound like—
respect they don't know how to say.

IV. The Reign Born from Rejection

You were never meant to be invited in.
You were meant to break the door off the frame.

Let their hate forge your discipline.
Let their doubt become your documentation.

Let every attempt to bury you—
drive your roots deeper.
Into soil they'll never stand on.

That's what Malcolm X did.
Jailed. Disowned. Hunted.
Not just by enemies—but by his own movement.

They feared his voice.
So he made it louder.

He didn't ask for a seat.
He rebuilt the structure.
And long after they tried to silence him—
he still speaks.

**"If you're not ready to die for it, put the word 'freedom' out of
your vocabulary."**
— *Malcolm X*

V. The Throne Built by Their Hate
"Hate becomes your reign."
— *Silent Threads*

You are not undone by hate.
You're defined by what it couldn't kill.

They tried to erase you—
but ended up engraving your name into legacy.

They fired every shot—
and watched you rise anyway.

Not just to stand.
To reign.

Let them talk.
Let them twist.
Let them aim low.

Because one day,
they will look up—
and realize:

They built your rise.
Not with loyalty.
Not with love.
But with every ounce of hate
That couldn't stop you.

That is your reign.
And their hate?

It didn't break you—
it built the steps to your throne.

SILENT AXIOM XX

"If you want to obtain more than you have, you must first become more than you are."
— *Silent Threads*

The Becoming Before the Crown

You don't wish for the rise.
You become the force that makes it inevitable.

Meaning:

Growth is required for gain.
The world does not reward potential—it rewards becoming.
You cannot hold more until you're built to carry more.
Expansion of results always follows the expansion of self.

Hidden Meaning:

The outer world mirrors the inner world.
You won't gain power, trust, impact, or legacy
until you've evolved into the version of yourself
that can bear the weight without breaking.

The reward isn't denied.
It's delayed—until you become the one who can carry it.

Message:
Transformation precedes elevation.
You want more?
Then become more.

The dream is real. But so is the cost.
You can't stay who you are
and expect to live at a level you haven't earned.

I. The Rise Isn't Granted. It's Engineered.
The rise isn't granted.
It's engineered.

It doesn't happen because you wish for it.
It doesn't come because you hope for it.
It arrives only when you've built the presence that commands it.

You don't chase elevation—
you forge the force that makes it inevitable.

II. The Capacity Before the Throne
You don't lack because life is unfair.
You lack because the weight of mastery
doesn't bow to untrained hands.

That crown you want?
It's too heavy for yo
u right now.

That title you crave?
Would crush you if it came too soon.

That respect you demand?
You haven't forged yourself into someone
who holds it effortlessly.

You want more?
Then build the spine that won't break under it.

The world isn't denying you—
it's waiting for the version of you
who can stand under the weight.

III. The Final Strike — No Mercy.

The world won't deny you.
It will test if you can hold what you asked for.

And if you can't?
It will break you first.

Success doesn't care how badly you want it.
It only bows to those who've earned
the strength to carry it.

This isn't about desire.
It's about weight.

And if you haven't built the hands—
then when the crown arrives,

it won't sit on your head.
It'll crush you instead.

IV. The Inky Johnson Collapse and Rebuild

Most people see the headlines.
Motivational speaker. NCAA star.
Stage presence. Raw passion. Big audience.

What they don't see?
The fracture.
The blood.
The moment his future snapped in half.

Inky Johnson was on his way to the NFL.
Dream set. Path clear. Millions waiting.
Then a hit—gone.
Paralyzed. Done.

Most people die in that moment.
Not him.

He didn't recover—he rebuilt.
Didn't just accept the pain—he converted it.
Didn't just speak—
he turned every word into a weapon for others to rise.

Inky didn't fold.
He became more.
So the world had no choice but to give him more.

V. The Becoming Before the Crown
**"If you want to obtain more than you have,
you must first become more than you are."**
— *Silent Threads*

Everything you want is real.
But not for the version of you standing still.
It's waiting for the version of you who earns it—

by how you wake up.
How you train.
How you lead.
How you take ownership of what you aren't yet—
and forge into what you need to be.

You don't get the crown first.
You become the weight that wears it.

And when that version shows up?

You don't chase the rise.
The rise bows to you.

CHAPTER CLOSING: THE CAGE IN ASH

You didn't escape the fire. You became it.

You don't walk back from fire like it never touched you. You don't return to comfort after you've felt what burns. And you sure as hell don't rebuild the same cage you just shattered.

You carry the weight now. Because everything weak in you? It's already been burned. What's left is forged—not polished. And it's ready.

The truth is this: if you made the cage, you can make the weapon. The same energy you used to shrink, to hide, to fold? That's the fire you now aim forward.

You used to mask the rage. You used to apologize for the heat. You used to crave comfort because it helped you forget what you could be. But that comfort cost you. And now? You're done paying for your own restraints.

The silence you lived in? That was never peace—it was potential, trapped. But now it speaks. Not in volume—but in weight. And the world is going to feel every ounce of it.

You are not a prisoner anymore. You are not potential waiting to be discovered. You are not someone hoping for approval before taking the next step.

You are the one who remembered what it felt like to be empty—and chose to fill yourself with fire instead.

You are not seeking applause. You are not asking for a path. You are not waiting for understanding.

You've trained in silence. You've bled without credit. You've sharpened in shadows.

So now?

Let them meet the version of you they were never prepared for.

And when they ask how you got here—when they wonder where you came from—when they scramble to understand the weight behind your presence?

You won't need to answer.

You'll be too busy walking over the ashes of your cage.

I. Queen Nzinga (1583 — Ndongo, Angola)
"Those who refuse to be ruled—must be trained to reign."
— *Attributed to Queen Nzinga*

She didn't inherit power.

She **took it**—after her brother failed and her people bled.

When the Portuguese came to colonize, she didn't flinch.

They denied her a chair at the negotiating table.

She made her servant into one—

and sat.

Back straight. Chin high. Unmoved.

Nzinga turned her body into a throne.

And her mind into a war machine.

She weaponized diplomacy.

Then **burned every bridge** when words failed.

She trained armies of women.

Forged alliances with former enemies.

Used religion as a tactic—**not a leash.**

They tried to cage her.
She turned the cage into a kingdom.

II. Shaka Senghor (1972 — Detroit, Michigan)
"I found peace the moment I stopped waiting for someone else to forgive me."
— *Shaka Senghor, TED Talk (2014)*

He pulled the trigger at nineteen.
Spent nineteen years behind bars.
Seven of those—in solitary.
No sound. No praise. No way out.

But instead of breaking—he rewired.
He didn't beg for forgiveness.
He **built himself into someone worth forgiving.**

Shaka turned his cage into curriculum.
His guilt into grit.
His pain into a **blueprint for redemption.**

He didn't talk loud.
He walked **heavy**.
And when the door finally opened—
he didn't run.
He carried the silence with him.

III. Final Battle Cry

You don't walk through hell just to survive.

You walk through it so no one forgets what lives on the other side.

Not inspiration.

Not permission.

Just pressure—refined.

I didn't come to inspire you.

I came to remind you what the fire feels like—and dare you to walk through it.

Ashes don't lie.

Walk like you burned it.

5

WHERE CHAINS STILL WHISPER

When Comfort Becomes the Cage

Freedom sounds beautiful until it demands something from you. This section is the heart of the prisoner's dilemma. We claim we want liberty. We shout about rights. But when freedom starts asking for sacrifice, most people trade it away in the name of convenience, comfort, or false security.

That's not betrayal. That's human nature at war with itself.

True freedom costs. It demands vigilance when you'd rather rest. It demands integrity when no one's watching. It demands standing when the crowd kneels.

That's why freedom isn't popular—it's terrifying. It removes the excuses. It removes the saviors. It removes the walls you used to blame for your weakness and tells you: now it's all on you.

And that's the real fear. Not captivity. But the unbearable weight of being fully responsible for your own life.

Most people don't want freedom. They want someone else to carry the risk. Someone else to choose. Someone else to fail. So they hand over their autonomy to systems, leaders, lovers, or illusions. And they convince themselves it's peace—when it's really a slow burial.

The ones who walk into freedom and keep walking? They've made peace with discomfort. They've learned to suffer clean. They've stopped begging for happiness and started protecting their sovereignty, no matter the cost.

Because freedom doesn't save you—it exposes you. Weaponize the sacrifice. Extract power from the pain. That's how you emerge from the ashes of grit.

SILENT AXIOM XXI

"Those that tell little white lies are color-blind to the truth."
— *Silent Threads*

Bending the Truth Doesn't Strengthen the Lie

When you blur the line, you stain the whole page.

Meaning:

Lies don't shrink by size—they corrode by nature. The moment you bend the truth, you compromise clarity, integrity, and power. You can't warp the facts and expect reality to hold.

Hidden Meaning:

You don't lose freedom in one blow—you lose it by degrees. A soft lie here. A silent omission there. Soon, you're not protecting peace—you're performing it. The moment you make peace with deception, you start erasing your own reflection.

Message / Takeaway:

Truth is the spine of freedom. Lie to others—you fracture connection. Lie to yourself—you dissolve your edge. Want power? Want peace? Then bleed for clarity. Speak what burns. Because silence wrapped in lies is the slowest form of self-erasure.

I. The First Lie Is Never the Last

We don't collapse into deceit—we slip.
A gentle excuse. A softened truth.
An omission framed as kindness.
But each bend weakens the backbone.
You say it's mercy—but it's maintenance.
And maintenance breeds performance.
And performance? It exhausts the soul.
So by the time the real test comes,
you've bent too far to stand.

II. The War Between Clarity and Comfort

Truth breaks things.
Relationships. Jobs. Egos. Illusions.
That's why lies win the easy rounds.
But comfort is a con.
It masks decay.
Freedom doesn't bloom in safety—
it rises from wreckage.
If you avoid speaking truth to protect the moment,
you forfeit the future.
And you will live under the rule
of those who lie better than you.

III. The Deception of "Little" Lies

"White lie."
Sounds clean. Sounds merciful.
But every lie wears armor.
It learns to survive.

You speak it once to dodge a hit—
then again to cover the dodge.
And now?
You're not just lying to them—
you're lying to yourself.
That's not strategy.
That's self-erasure with a polite mask.

IV. Malcolm X Didn't Whisper

He wasn't feared because he lied—
he was feared because he *didn't*.
He called truth what it was:
Uncomfortable. Uninvited. Unapologetic.
They called it dangerous.
They called him radical.
But clarity, when wielded boldly, always is.

**"I'm for truth, no matter who tells it. I'm for justice, no matter who
it's for or against."**
— *Malcolm X, Ford Hall Forum, 1963*

He didn't polish his truth for comfort.
He weaponized it.
And that's what made him impossible to silence.

V. The Lie You Call "White" Still Bleeds You Gray
"Those that tell little white lies are color-blind to the truth."
— *Silent Threads*

You think it's small.
A mercy. A buffer. A peacekeeper.
But the truth you hide today
becomes the fracture you trip on tomorrow.

Lie enough, and clarity turns to static.
Purpose fades into performance.
And conviction?
It gets diluted with every "just this once."

Don't confuse kindness with convenience.
Don't trade your edge for applause.
The world doesn't need more soft lies.
It needs sharp truth—
cut clean.
Spoken once.
And owned without apology.

So bleed it.
Even when it stings.
Especially when it matters.
Because truth is heavy.
But lies will hollow you out.

SILENT AXIOM XXII

"It's better to suffer at the hands of a monster than endure the darkness of an angel."
— *Silent Threads*

The Beautiful Ones Kill Quietly

Not all danger screams. Some seduce.

Meaning:

You can fight the enemy you recognize. But the most dangerous betrayal comes wrapped in beauty, charm, or care. What you can name, you can resist. What you trust—can destroy you.

Hidden Meaning:

The true threat isn't always claws and growls—it's care with conditions. Some manipulate through mercy. They don't crush you with rage—they own you with kindness. And by the time you realize it? You've handed them the leash. Angels with agendas are the architects of captivity.

Message / Takeaway:

Don't confuse softness with safety. Don't mistake control for care. The greatest threat to your freedom might be the one telling you they're protecting it. The monster scars the skin. The angel steals the soul. And only one teaches you to bow while smiling.

I. Not All Kindness Is Clean

Control doesn't always look like a fist.
Sometimes it looks like flattery.
Praise with strings.
Support with ceilings.
They love you—until you evolve.
They uplift you—but only in the direction they choose.
That's not love.
That's leverage.
And when you grow past them,
you'll feel the shift:
The cold withdrawal.
The subtle guilt.
The pressure to shrink back.
That's when you'll realize—
you were never held.
You were being handled.

II. Monsters Are Easier to Fight Than Angels

A monster announces itself.
It's loud. Violent. Clear.
You can swing at it.
Bleed from it.
Know what you're up against.

But the angel?
It soothes you into surrender.
Smiles while silencing you.
Loves you into obedience.
You won't even realize you're in a cage—

until you stop breathing.

Some pain wears perfume.
And that's why you never saw it coming.

III. Don't Confuse Safety with Surrender

They'll call you "too intense."
"Too cold."
"Too much."
But all you're doing is protecting your sovereignty.
They want access—not understanding.
Obedience—not respect.

Let them talk.
Because if your clarity makes them uncomfortable,
they were never here for your freedom.

IV. Joan of Arc Burned for Refusing to Bow

She didn't fall in battle.
She was betrayed in robes.
Set up by leaders who claimed to protect her.
Judged by men too small for her fire.
They disguised cowardice as sanctity.
Lit the flames—and whispered prayers.

"I am not afraid... I was born to do this."
— Joan of Arc, Rouen Trial Transcripts, 1431

She saw through their scripture.
Saw the truth beneath their rituals.
And chose to burn—rather than bow to their illusion of light.

V. The Beautiful Ones Kill Quietly
"It's better to suffer at the hands of a monster than endure the darkness of an angel."
— *Silent Threads*

Some call you "love" while stealing your voice.
Some cover your eyes while claiming to protect them.
They'll sell you comfort—and hand you chains.

So when the touch feels soft but the fire in you dims—
pause.
Look again.

Because real love doesn't condition your freedom.
Real support doesn't soften your strength.
And real protection never requires permission to grow.

The monster is loud.
But the angel?
The angel buries you—smiling.

When you finally stop asking to be seen...
When you stop explaining your boundaries...
You don't become cold.
You become clear.

And the next time darkness wears a smile—
you'll see the fangs.
And you won't flinch.
Because lions don't kneel for angels.

They just watch—
and wait for the lie to speak first.

SILENT AXIOM XXIII

"A lion is never threatened by the calamity of hyenas."
— *Silent Threads*

Stillness Before the Strike

Lions don't roar to remind you who they are.
They just wait—then remove the threat.

Meaning:
Noise doesn't rattle those who've mastered stillness.
Hyenas bark because they're unsure.
Lions don't.
The apex doesn't entertain chaos—
it watches, calculates, and strikes
when the moment serves the mission.

Hidden Meaning:
A lion doesn't waste time explaining itself to scavengers.
It doesn't defend its throne with noise.
Its power isn't proven through bark—it's felt through movement.
The pack makes noise because it fears what silence might do next.
And that's the difference:
Noise reacts. Presence reigns.

Message / Takeaway:
You've explained enough.
You've played humble for the comfort of the loud.

Let them circle.
Let them scream.
Let them confuse silence for submission.
Because what they don't know is this:
You're not frozen.
You're focused.
And when the time comes?
You won't argue.
You'll execute.

I. Hyenas Need the Crowd

They don't attack alone.
They perform—for each other.
Noise is their safety net.
Distraction is their tactic.
They want to pull you from your position.
To get you barking back.
To make you defend what doesn't need defending.
They don't want your throne.
They want your focus.
Don't descend.
Don't engage.
You lose nothing by letting them talk—
but everything if you try to prove you're still the lion.

II. The Lion Doesn't Flinch

The lion doesn't roar for attention.
It doesn't react to every insult.
It waits—perfectly still.

Because power doesn't perform.
It doesn't panic.
It moves when movement is final.
That's strength:
Unbothered.
Unapologetic.
Undeniable.

III. You Owe Them Nothing

Let them misread your silence.
Let them call it weakness.
Let them think you're asleep.
Because silence isn't surrender—
it's setup.
When you roar, it's not for noise—
it's for closure.
Every second you stay silent?
You're sharpening.
You're aiming.
You're preparing the move that ends the game.
And when you move—
they'll never see it coming.

IV. Harriet Tubman Walked in Stillness

She didn't raise her voice.
She didn't announce the mission.
She *moved*—
through death traps, betrayal, and blood.
Quiet. Tactical. Relentless.

She didn't argue with masters.
She outmaneuvered them.

"I never ran my train off the track, and I never lost a passenger."
— *Harriet Tubman, as recorded by Sarah Bradford,* Scenes in the Life of
Harriet Tubman, *1869*

Surrounded by hyenas—
she moved like the lion.
Not with noise.
But with results.

V. Stillness Before the Strike
"A lion is never threatened by the calamity of hyenas."
— *Silent Threads*

Let them circle.
Let them mock what they fear.
Let them confuse silence for submission.

Because real power doesn't flinch.
It calculates.
And when it moves—
it doesn't bark.
It *ends* the noise.

You've outgrown the need to be understood.
Now you operate in stillness.
Now you move once—
and that's all it takes.

Hyenas bark.
Lions feed.

SILENT AXIOM XXIV

"If you believe courage requires strength, wait until you discover fear."
— *Silent Threads*

Courage Was Never Clean

Fear isn't the enemy.
It's the forge.

Meaning:
Fear doesn't weaken you—it reveals you.
Courage isn't found in the absence of fear.
It's born from fire *inside* it.
The more fear you face,
the more conviction it takes to keep standing.
That's not weakness.
That's real courage.

Hidden Meaning:
Strength lifts weight.
Fear *decides* if you'll carry it.
Courage isn't for the strongest—
it's for the ones who won't bow
when everything screams "run."
It doesn't rise before fear—
it's *created* by it.

Conviction doesn't start clean.
It starts cracked, bleeding, trembling—
and still moving.

Message / Takeaway:
You don't need to feel ready.
You don't need to be fearless.
You just need to *move* inside the fear.
Because when the pressure hits—
those who run aren't weak.
They're just not willing to choose.

I. Fear Is the Test, Not the Enemy

Courage isn't unshakable.
It isn't poetic.
It's dirty. It's raw.
It's choosing not to run when *every cell* begs you to fold.
It's stepping forward while crying, while broken, while unsure.
That's not failure—
that's entry.
Fear is the gate.
Most never pass it.
Because it doesn't feel noble.
It feels like death.
And that's exactly why it's real.

II. Pain Will Show You What You Really Worship

Pain doesn't lie.
It doesn't care who you pretend to be.

When it rips through you—
only the truth survives.
Fear strips the costume.
Strips the branding.
Strips the pride.
What's left?
You.
And if you're not grounded,
you'll vanish before the fire even starts.
Because pain only answers one question:
Will you stay when it hurts?

III. Courage Isn't Born in Fire—It's Born in Decision

You don't rise because you feel ready.
You rise because *you refuse to stay down.*
Courage isn't instinct.
It's *choice.*
Made again.
And again.
While shaking.
While bleeding.
While *not knowing* how the story ends.
It's not poetic—
it's brutal.
And that's why it matters.

IV. Desmond Doss Stood Without a Rifle

World War II. Okinawa.
Bullets flying.

Men dying.
And one medic—*no weapon*—stepped into hell.
Desmond Doss refused to kill.
Not because he was soft—
because he was *built different*.
He pulled seventy-five men off that ridge
with nothing but his hands.
And a prayer.

"Please Lord, help me get one more."
— *Desmond Doss, 1945*

He didn't stand because he wasn't afraid.
He stood because they needed him—
and fear wasn't enough to stop him.

V. Courage Was Never Clean
**"If you believe courage requires strength,
wait until you discover fear."**
— *Silent Threads*

Courage doesn't arrive with clarity.
It shows up shaking.
It stands in silence—
when the screaming is inside you.

Stop waiting to feel brave.
That moment doesn't come.

It's never clean.
Never polished.
Never timed just right.

It's ugly.
It's violent.
It *burns*.

And still—
you rise.
You walk anyway.
You move inside the fire.
Not because you're strong—
but because the mission is stronger than your fear.

That's courage.
And it doesn't need applause.
It just needs *you*—
to choose.

SILENT AXIOM XXV

"Never sacrifice freedom for the complacency of happiness."
— *Silent Threads*

The Cage That Feeds You

Comfort isn't peace.
It's the prettiest prison of all.

Meaning:

Comfort seduces.
It promises happiness, ease, and rest—
but erodes your fire one soft day at a time.
You don't lose freedom all at once.
You lose it smiling.

Hidden Meaning:

What you call "happiness" may just be sedation.
You didn't get weak because life broke you.
You got weak because you stopped choosing the sharp path.
Complacency doesn't kill loudly.
It just numbs—until you forget you had teeth.

Message / Takeaway:

You can't be free and sedated.
You can't be sharp and soft.
You can't grow and stay safe.
So choose.

But never lie to yourself and pretend you can have both.

I. The Lie of the Soft Life
They say you've earned it.
The rest.
The peace.
The reward.
So you sit.
You breathe easy.
And you stop asking questions.
Stop chasing your edge.
Stop becoming.
Until one day—
that stillness doesn't feel sacred.
It feels like a cage you called "peace."

II. The Cage Comes with Pillows
You don't notice the bars at first.
Because it's cozy.
They praise your caution.
They call you "wise" for not risking.
But slowly,
the walls close in.
Not with violence—
with comfort.
And by the time you look up,
you've traded fire for routine.
You didn't die.
You faded.

III. Slavery in Modern Terms Is Voluntary

No one's forcing you anymore.

They don't have to.

Just hand you a salary,

a soft bed,

a few likes—

and you'll build your own cell.

Worse?

You'll defend it.

Call anyone who rattles the bars "reckless."

Call your numbness "success."

But deep down—

you know better.

IV. Søren Kierkegaard Refused to Be Comfortable

He had the option:

Marriage. Fame. Applause.

He walked away.

Because Søren Kierkegaard understood what most ignore:

Ease is expensive—

it costs clarity.

So he wrote in exile.

Mocked. Alone.

But *free.*

**"People demand freedom of speech as a compensation
for the freedom of thought which they seldom use."**

— *Søren Kierkegaard*

He didn't chase comfort.
He chased conviction.
And he paid the price —
in solitude.
But not in regret.

V. The Cage That Feeds You
"Never sacrifice freedom for the complacency of happiness."
— *Silent Threads*

The world doesn't need to chain you.
It just needs to keep you *comfortable*.
And once you've accepted the lie —
that happiness is the goal,
not growth —
you'll shrink.
And then justify the shrinking.
Because the cage?
It feeds you.
But what it feeds you —
costs your edge.
Your fire.
Your becoming.

Don't call that "peace."
Call it what it is:

A slow death with silk sheets.

CHAPTER CLOSING: THE COST OF FREEDOM

The chain doesn't have to cut—it just has to comfort.

Freedom isn't soft. It doesn't come wrapped in comfort or praise. It doesn't arrive gently or knock politely. Freedom walks in like fire and demands to know what you're willing to burn to keep it. And most people—despite what they claim—aren't willing to burn much at all.

They sell it early. For applause. For ease. For the illusion of control. Not in some grand betrayal, but in small moments of convenience. A bent truth here. A silent nod there. The lie isn't loud. It's subtle. It sounds like: "It's not worth the fight," or, "This isn't the right time," or, "Don't make it harder than it has to be."

That's how it starts.

You begin to perform freedom instead of living it. You decorate your cage. You rationalize the cost. You tell yourself you're free because there are no bars in sight—but the chains are still there. They don't clang. They don't cut deep. They cushion. They praise your quiet. They reward your compromise. And that's why they work.

Because they don't feel like chains.

Real freedom is something else entirely. It's raw. It's costly. It will ask you to give up the crowd. To disappoint those who preferred the obedient version of you. To sacrifice comfort in exchange for clarity. And it will not give you certainty in return. There are no guarantees with freedom—only the responsibility to claim it, moment by moment, inch by inch.

It won't always feel like victory. Sometimes it will feel like loss. Like loneliness. Like standing alone in a storm while others gather inside, warm and blind. But if you can endure that, if you can choose truth over ease, presence over performance, conviction over approval—then you begin to understand what freedom actually is.

It's not a gift. It's not a right. It's a decision. A costly, painful, inconvenient decision to stay true to yourself no matter how much the world begs you to flinch.

If you think you're free because no one's holding a chain—you're already owned.

I. Toussaint Louverture — The General Born in Chains

Born enslaved in 1743,
Toussaint Louverture didn't wait for freedom.
He became it.

He didn't lead politely.
Didn't win popularity contests.
He shattered three empires with nothing but discipline, clarity,
and an iron refusal to bow.

Napoleon offered peace.
Toussaint refused the lie.

They locked him in a frozen cell—
but he had already freed a nation.

"I was born a slave, but nature gave me the soul of a free man."
— *Toussaint Louverture*

His spine rewrote the world map.
The chains that bound him now rust in soil he made sovereign.

II. Václav Havel — The Playwright Who Refused to Lie

Born in 1936 under the rise of Soviet control,
Havel never raised his voice—
but his silence was honest.

In a country ruled by censors,
he wrote truth.

And for that, they locked him away.
He came back—not with revenge,
but with clarity.

He became president.
Not because he sought power,
but because he never sold out to keep peace.

"The salvation of this human world lies nowhere else than in the human heart."
— *Václav Havel*

Freedom doesn't always march.
Sometimes it waits—
unbending. Uncompromised.

And when the cage collapses,
it steps forward—already prepared to lead.

III. The Fire Beneath Peace

The truly free have learned to ignore noise.
They don't react to every bark,
every opinion,
every scream for attention.

The apex doesn't answer chaos—it studies it.
Then moves once.
Precisely.
Decisively.

Fear will come.
Not the kind that startles—
the kind that stalks.
The kind that demands you stand
without backup,
without applause.

That's where courage is born.
Not in the absence of fear—
but **inside it.**

Comfort will try to seduce you.
It will offer smiles, predictability, pleasure.

But it will quietly steal your edge,
dull your instincts,
and leave you domesticated.

And once you've lost the fire?
You'll call the cage home.

IV. The Cost of Freedom

Freedom is chaos—mastered.
It is responsibility—sharpened into refusal.

The threads you pull will either strangle you—
or set you free.

Choose wisely.

No cheer.
No applause.
Just spine.
Just clarity.
Just choice.

Freedom isn't handed—it's clawed back.
One refusal at a time.

And if it doesn't cost you something?
It was never freedom to begin with.

THE PRISONER UNLEASHED

This Is Your Reckoning

MARKED BY TIME

Freedom is chaos mastered.

The threads you pull will either strangle you or set you free.
Freedom doesn't shake hands.
It doesn't whisper sweet nothings about balance and patience.

Freedom invades.
It kicks down the damn door and demands sacrifice.
It's not here to make you comfortable.
It's here to test what you're made of.

And most?
They fold.
They give it away for applause.
For convenience.
For control wrapped in velvet lies.
Not with one grand betrayal—

but in tiny, gutless moments:
A nod they didn't believe in.
A truth they twisted.
A silence they justified.
The lie? It never roars.
It whispers.

▼ *"This isn't the right time."*
▼ *"Why risk everything?"*
▼ *"Just play the part. Win later."*

That's how it begins.
You start *performing* freedom—
instead of **living** it.

You dress up your cage.
Hang degrees on the wall.
Smile for cameras.
And convince yourself:
"I'm free—look, no bars."

But those chains?
Still there.
No rattle. No blood.
Just soft, padded obedience.

They clap for your silence.
They celebrate your restraint.
And that's what makes them deadly—
because they **feel safe.**

THE COST THAT COMES WITH TRUTH

Freedom isn't handed out like candy.

It's not ceremonial.

It's not some polished quote framed on a wall.

It's earned. In blood. In sweat. In solitude.

And it will cost you.

More than you want to pay.

▼ The crowd's approval.

▼ The easy smiles of people who loved the tame version of you.

▼ The illusions that helped you sleep.

It'll strip you of certainty.

It'll hand you choices with no spotlight.

It'll lock you in a room with your reflection

and dare you not to blink.

Freedom is not for the faint.

It's not your inheritance.

It's your war.

Every inch must be taken.

Every battle earned by:

▼ Clarity.

▼ Discipline.

▼ Defiance.

THE FINAL STRIKE

You weren't gifted extra time.
You weren't handed a vault to dip into when life got hard.

You got minutes.
And they vanished while you planned, paused, and waited.

Time doesn't care.
It doesn't owe you.
It doesn't make deals.
It's a silent thief.

It takes while you hesitate.
It steals while you chase comfort.
It robs you blind with distractions dressed as duty.

No alarms. No apologies. Just absence.
Like the moment right before night swallows the sky.

The tragedy?
Not that time is limited.
But that you were convinced you controlled it.

That if you suffered now, joy would come later.
That sacrifice today meant redemption tomorrow.

It won't.
Time doesn't barter.
It just moves.

So the question isn't:
Do you have time left?
The question is:
What the hell will remain when it's gone?

Will it be a pile of regrets and empty performances?
Or a version of you that didn't flinch?
Didn't fold?
Didn't beg for permission?

A version that bled—but **built**.
That burned—but **became**.
That staggered—but **stood**.

THIS BOOK ISN'T YOUR SALVATION. YOU ARE.

Let's get something straight.
This book?
It's not your shield.
It's not your map.
It's not your damn rescue.

You are.

When you close this page—
the world won't stop spinning.
The clock won't freeze.

But now...
Let time try to take from you.

Because you?
You'll take back something more:
the right to stand unchained.
Unapologetic.
Unbroken.
Reborn.

DAY SEVEN. NO MERCY.

There's no rest for your resurrection.

You made it this far.
Through the noise.
Through the silence.
Through the breaking.

And now you want to breathe.

But this isn't the exhale.
This is the warpath.

And you don't get mercy when you've just risen from the grave.

You get one choice:
Finish the fight.

And if you're wondering what follows....

I. My Final Threads – "What Follows"

This is me, talking directly to you.
These aren't just words.

This ink?
It bled from my very eyes.
These pages?
They carry my scars.

This book is a symbol—of pain, of experience, and proof that you can rise.

I've been right where you're at.
I know what it feels like to fall.
But I also know what it takes to ascend.

My words are truth.
But truth alone won't save you.

You must embrace the pain.
You must wield its power.

Why are you here?
Was it just the book cover that captured you?
How did you fall so far from ambition?

I'll tell you why....

You're no victim.
You surrendered.
You retreated.
You failed.

You let comfort seduce you.
You allowed weakness to infect your volition.
You drank from the fountains of their disdain.

This isn't about being "Alpha" or "Beta."
This is about how you let the noise—inside and out—suffocate your fire.

Now you stand at my line.
And you've got a decision to make.

Do you cling to the status quo?
Do you allow failure to define you?
Do you keep letting this hollow culture of false empowerment and out-of-control political correct-ness shape your identity?

I don't give a damn about your politics.
I care about what you represent.

And whether you like it or not—
we're in this together.

So...

Are you ready to OWN it?
Embrace your failure.
Fuel your scars.

Because now—we're about to redefine your triumph.

HERE'S YOUR CHALLENGE:

Get your shit together.
Lace up your boots—or your high heels. Doesn't matter.
What matters… is your commitment to come back—harder.

You asked: *What's next? What follows?*

Now that you have your blueprint—
the rest is on you.

But my words are here—*here to guide you.*

Collect your thoughts.
Sharpen your tools.

Consume their misguided self-doubt.
Channel their flailing insecurity.
Turn every weapon they throw at you into ammunition.
Let that be your fuel.

Because it's not just the climb—
it's the transformation.

Your next battle?
It's not en route—it's HERE.

Follow this blueprint.
Your new shadows await.

They wait...
for your **Path to Reign.**

Close the book—while cowards sleep.

"Reclaim your kingdom—
you've got a battlefield to command."

— Mr. Krush

Coming Soon

The Path to Reign:
No One Will Save You

"Desire isn't enough for reign.
You must bleed for it."

~ Mr. Krush, The Path to Reign

ABOUT THE AUTHOR

Eric M. Kilcullen is a veteran, medical student, and founder of Ink & Armour Publishing. After years of walking through fire—military deployments, clinical training, and personal loss—he forged his voice into something sharper than silence. His writing blends discipline, defiance, and raw human truth. He is currently completing his doctorate in naturopathic medicine at Sonoran University of Health Science, where he advocates for integrity in both healing and leadership.

When he's not writing, you'll find him rebuilding engines, raising hell in the gym, or quietly charting the next move. Reign isn't a crown—it's a code.

THE CODEX OF CHAOS

Every Thread Has Teeth.

CHAPTER 1: THE PREDATOR OF CHAOS

Opening: Silence is the deadliest force against chaos.
This section reveals how power hides in stillness, not noise.

1. **"Silence remains the predator to chaos."**
   Meaning: Chaos feeds on noise.
   Hidden Meaning: Silence is not weakness—it is focused force.
   Message: True control never announces itself.

2. **"To shun adventure is to deny yourself a life worth living."**
   Meaning: Risk is the seed of growth.
   Hidden Meaning: Most people die before they ever live.
   Message: Discomfort is your doorway to purpose.

3. **"You cannot understand the depths of violence without first mastering the power of silence."**
   Meaning: Chaos without control is destruction.
   Hidden Meaning: Master silence, and you master the strike.
   Message: Power requires discipline before impact.

4. **"Where you see change, I discovered growth."**
   Meaning: Disruption is often evolution in disguise.
   Hidden Meaning: Growth is never comfortable.
   Message: Reframe discomfort as your next chapter.

5. **"Life's forks are conquered best with allies."**
   Meaning: Strength multiplies through trust.
   Hidden Meaning: The lone wolf bleeds quietly.
   Message: Loyalty sharpens direction.

   Closing: Every warrior begins in silence—not because they are weak, but because their strike is being forged.

CHAPTER 2: BROKEN & BOUND

Opening: This section explores the silent shackles we wear. Not all scars are visible—some are inherited, others self-forged.

6. **"If it's revenge you're after, begin with the version of you who betrayed your potential."**
   Meaning: The first enemy is always internal.
   Hidden Meaning: Betrayal begins within.
   Message: Reclaim what you gave away.

7. **"Even the sharpest teeth cannot bite water."**
   Meaning: Brute strength is useless without timing.
   Hidden Meaning: Flow outlasts force.
   Message: Flexibility is survival.

8. **"Our hands can create anything but time."**
   Meaning: Time is your most fragile resource.
   Hidden Meaning: Lost time is self-betrayal.
   Message: Guard it like your last breath.

9. **"One must fight darkness until it bleeds light."**
   Meaning: Peace is earned, not granted.
   Hidden Meaning: Resistance reveals power.
   Message: Don't make peace—take it.

10. **"Spare no sympathy for self-inflicted wounds."**
    Meaning: Accountability is the first step to reign.
    Hidden Meaning: Pain without ownership is poison.
    Message: Fix the break, or repeat it.

    Closing: Chains can look like comfort. This section tears them off, link by link, until all that's left is will.

CHAPTER 3: THE SURVIVOR'S CODE
Opening: These aren't just lessons—they're survival blueprints. The unspoken rules of those who keep standing when the smoke clears.

11. **"It's not death I'm chasing—I'm simply trying to survive your way of life."**
    Meaning: Survival is resistance, not submission.
    Hidden Meaning: Conformity can kill you slowly.
    Message: Protect your identity at all costs.

12. **"I didn't build the bridge for my enemies to succeed—I built it to learn from their mistakes."**
Meaning: Learn even from the ones who wish you harm.
Hidden Meaning: Every failure is a map.
Message: Study your enemy and surpass them.

13. **"Do not allow victory to become your defeat—success has no limits."**
Meaning: Growth ends when comfort begins.
Hidden Meaning: Yesterday's win is today's weakness if you stop.
Message: Always be in pursuit.

14. **"The greatest opportunities are forged from the ashes of compromise."**
Meaning: Destruction clears the path for rebirth.
Hidden Meaning: Sometimes loss is the gift.
Message: Collapse is construction in disguise.

15. **"In the shadow of a hero, a coward endures."**
Meaning: Not all who walk beside you are built like you.
Hidden Meaning: Loyalty must be tested—not assumed.
Message: Proximity doesn't prove purpose.

Closing: Survival isn't breath—it's defiance. These codes are the bones of the unbreakable.

CHAPTER 4: HIDDEN CAGES

Opening: These are the traps you didn't know you stepped into. They look like success. They sound like comfort. They move like safety. But they're bars all the same.

16. **"Confusing volume for weight is how the weak mistake the strong."**
    Meaning: Loud doesn't mean powerful.
    Hidden Meaning: Empty barrels make the most noise.
    Message: Depth always defeats drama.

17. **"Success bows to three forces—Education, Experience, and Exposure."**
    Meaning: Power is earned through learning and lived proof.
    Hidden Meaning: Skipping steps weakens your throne.
    Message: Build on truth—not trend.

18. **"To quench a shark's thirst—feed it blood."**
    Meaning: You can't ignore your nature.
    Hidden Meaning: Hunger transforms into destruction—or direction.
    Message: Master the beast before it masters you.

19. **"Their hate became my reign."**
    Meaning: Let their venom build your crown.
    Hidden Meaning: Hate is energy. Use it.
    Message: If it doesn't break you—make it elevate you.

20. **"If you want to obtain more than you have, you must first become more than you are."**
    Meaning: Growth is a prerequisite to greatness.
    Hidden Meaning: Your internal shift unlocks external change.
    Message: Become before you conquer.

Closing: Your cage was never built by them. You built it, named it comfort, and sat inside. Now—break out.

CHAPTER V: THE COST OF FREEDOM

Opening: Freedom is expensive. And most aren't willing to pay. This section reveals the true price—not just of liberation, but of becoming.

21. **"Those that tell little white lies are color-blind to the truth."**
    Meaning: All lies bleed the same.
    Hidden Meaning: Deception starts small—then rots everything.
    Message: Don't flirt with dishonor. Truth is war.

22 **"It's better to suffer at the hands of a monster than endure the darkness of an angel."**
    Meaning: Open evil is less dangerous than hidden betrayal.
    Hidden Meaning: Beauty blinds more than brutality.
    Message: Learn the mask. Trust your instinct.

23. **"A lion is never threatened by the calamity of hyenas."**
    Meaning: Noise is a distraction.
    Hidden Meaning: Power needs no permission—and no performance.
    Message: Hold your ground. Let them bark.

24. **"If you believe courage requires strength, wait until you discover fear."**
    Meaning: Fear is the birthplace of courage.
    Hidden Meaning: Strength is forged through fear—not after it.
    Message: Walk through fire—don't wait for it to cool.

25. **"Never sacrifice freedom for the complacency of happiness."**
    Meaning: Comfort is the deadliest cage.
    Hidden Meaning: Joy without purpose will sedate your potential.
    Message: Choose purpose—even if it hurts.

"And when silence is all that remains, you'll see the truth—for only in discomfort can you grow beyond the complacency that has made you prisoner to the chaos you fear."

-Mr. Krush